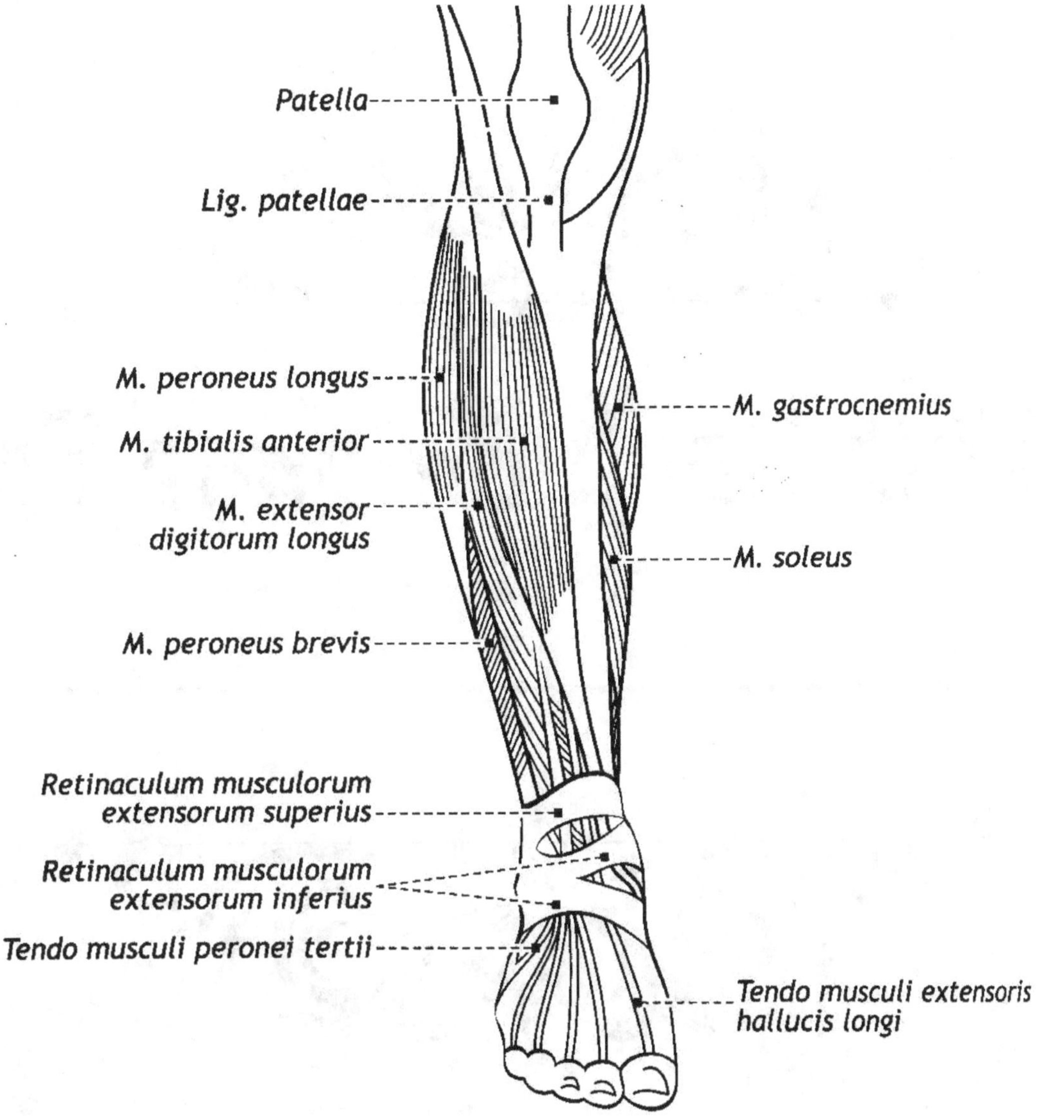
Patella
Lig. patellae
M. peroneus longus
M. tibialis anterior
M. extensor digitorum longus
M. peroneus brevis
Retinaculum musculorum extensorum superius
Retinaculum musculorum extensorum inferius
Tendo musculi peronei tertii
M. gastrocnemius
M. soleus
Tendo musculi extensoris hallucis longi

This Book Belongs To

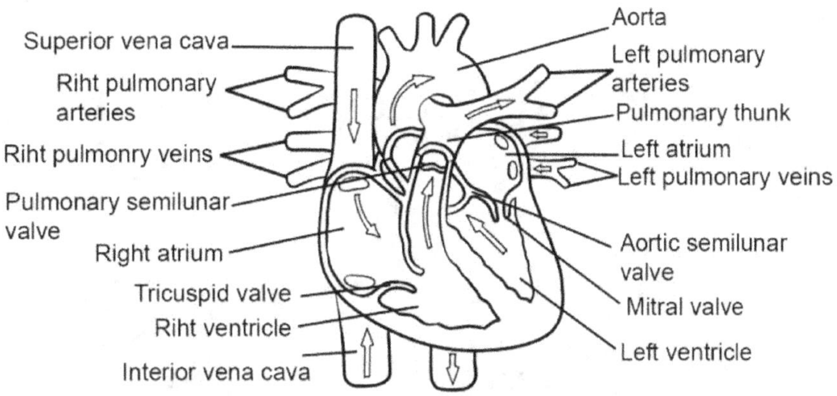

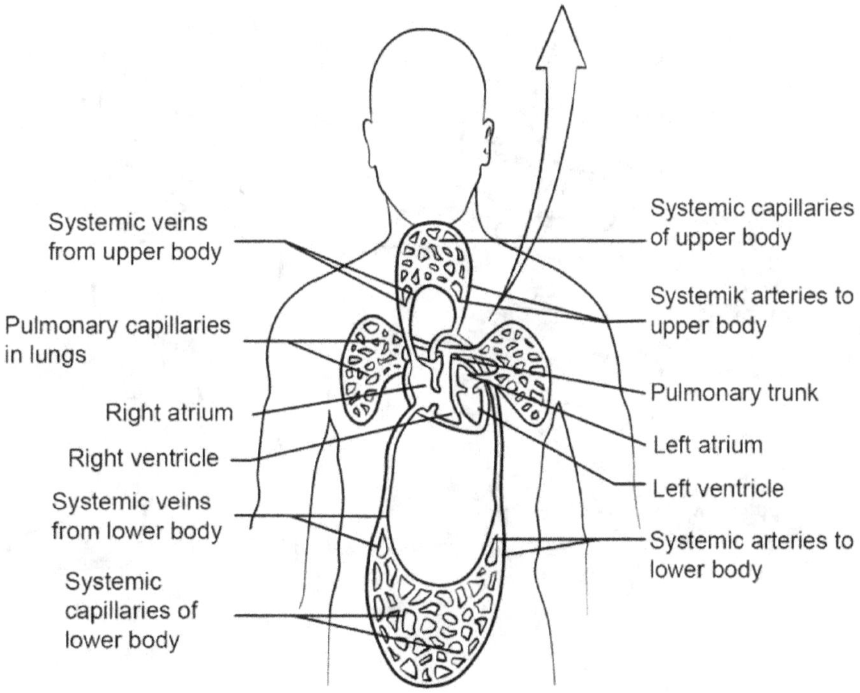

Human Circulatory System

Color the Digestive Tract

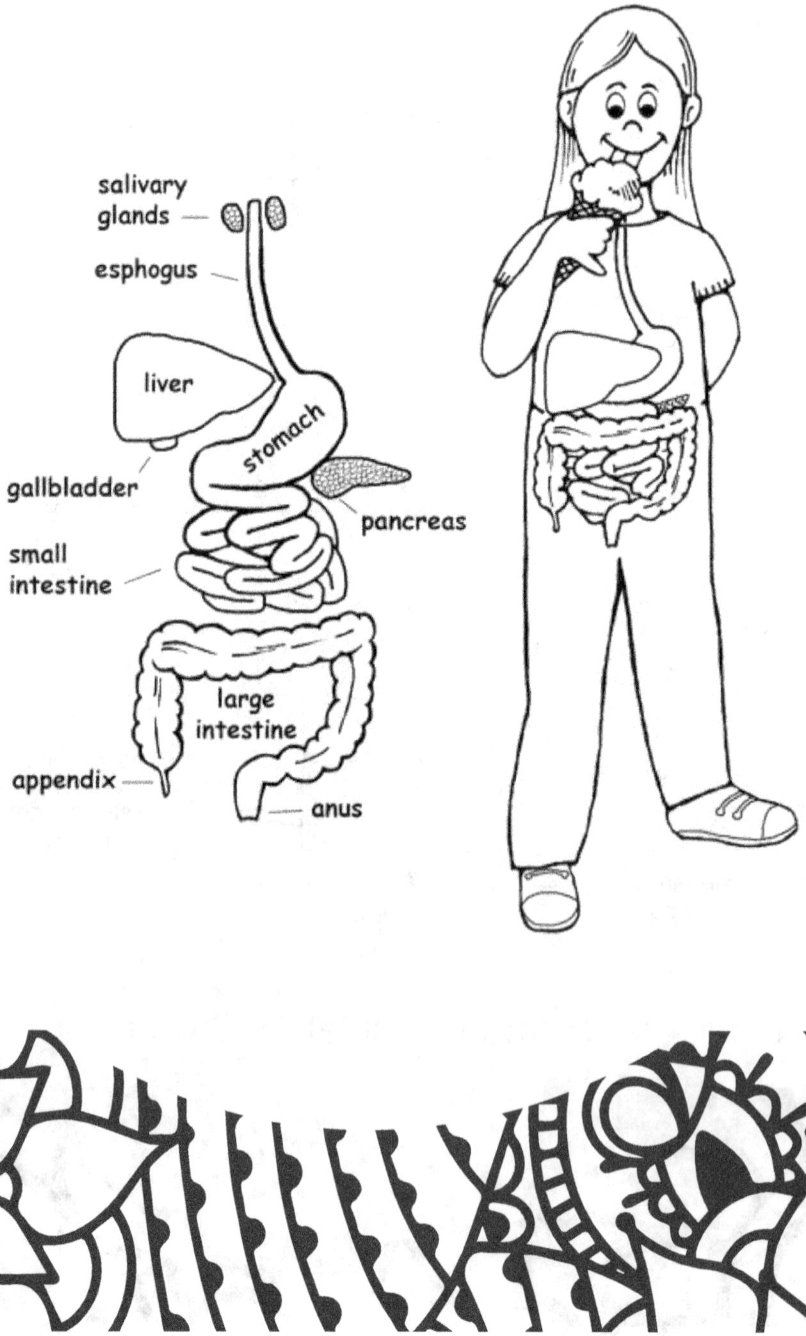

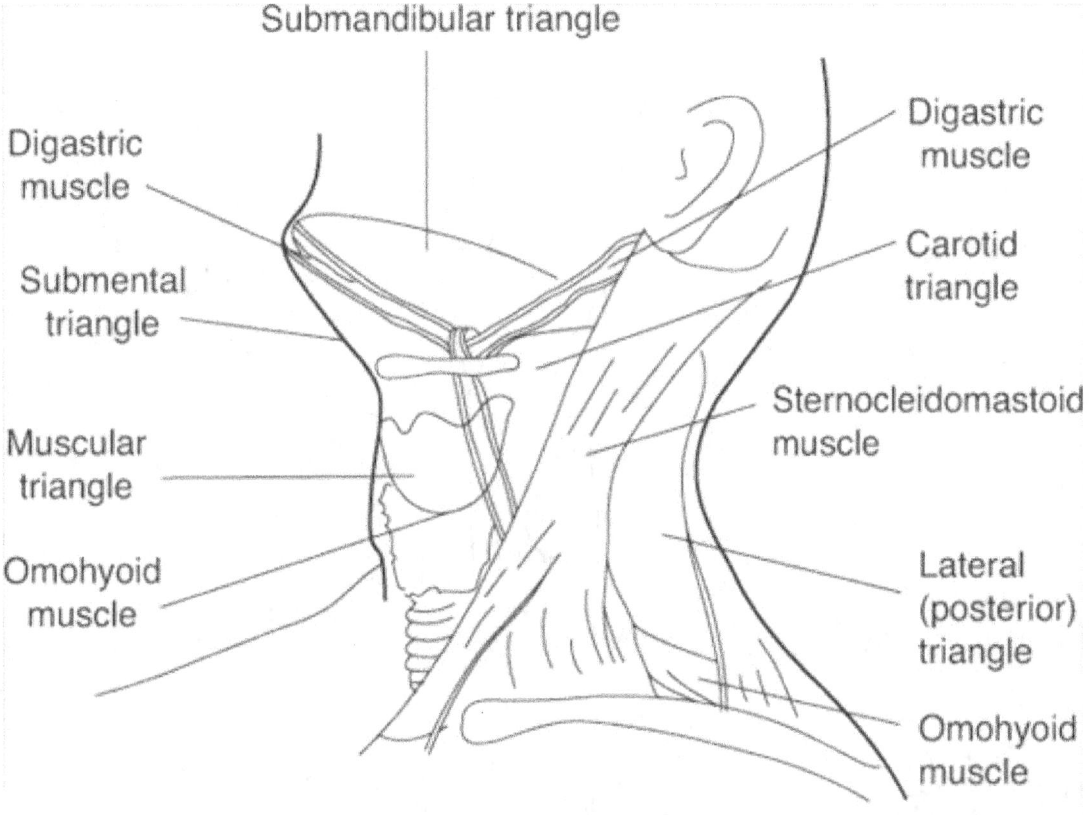
Submandibular triangle
Digastric muscle
Submental triangle
Muscular triangle
Omohyoid muscle
Digastric muscle
Carotid triangle
Sternocleidomastoid muscle
Lateral (posterior) triangle
Omohyoid muscle

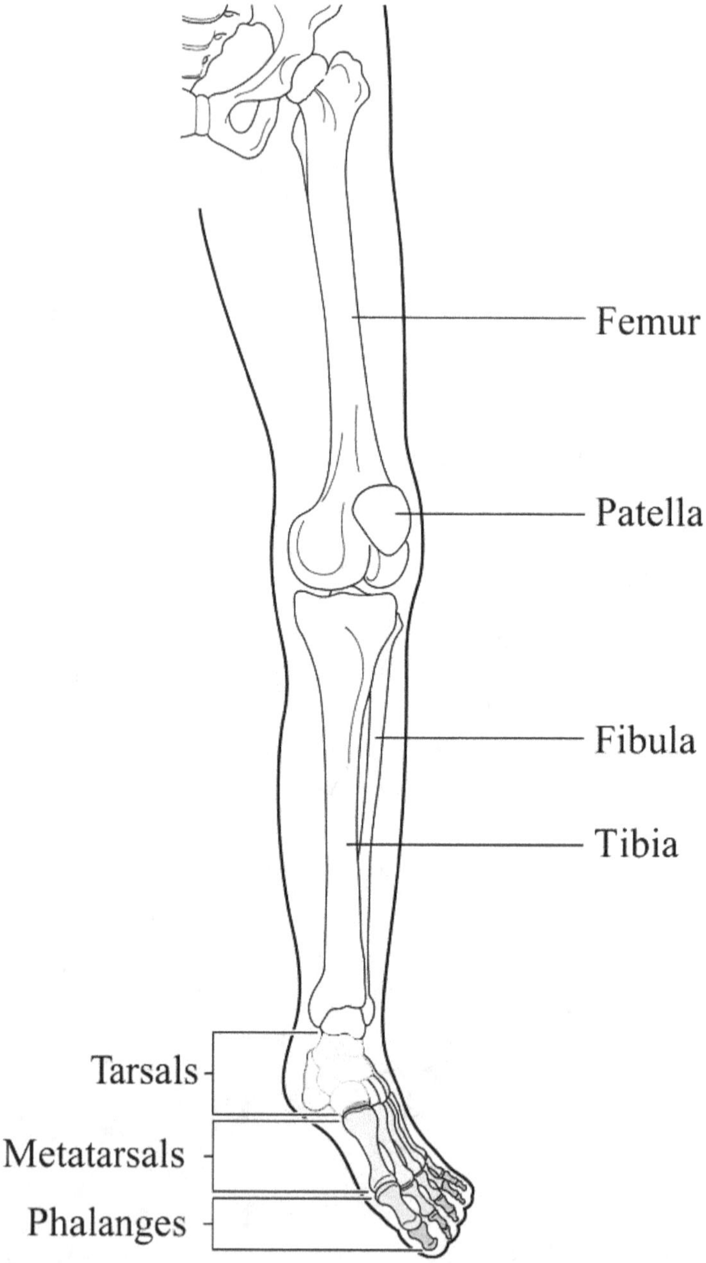
Femur
Patella
Fibula
Tibia
Tarsals
Metatarsals
Phalanges

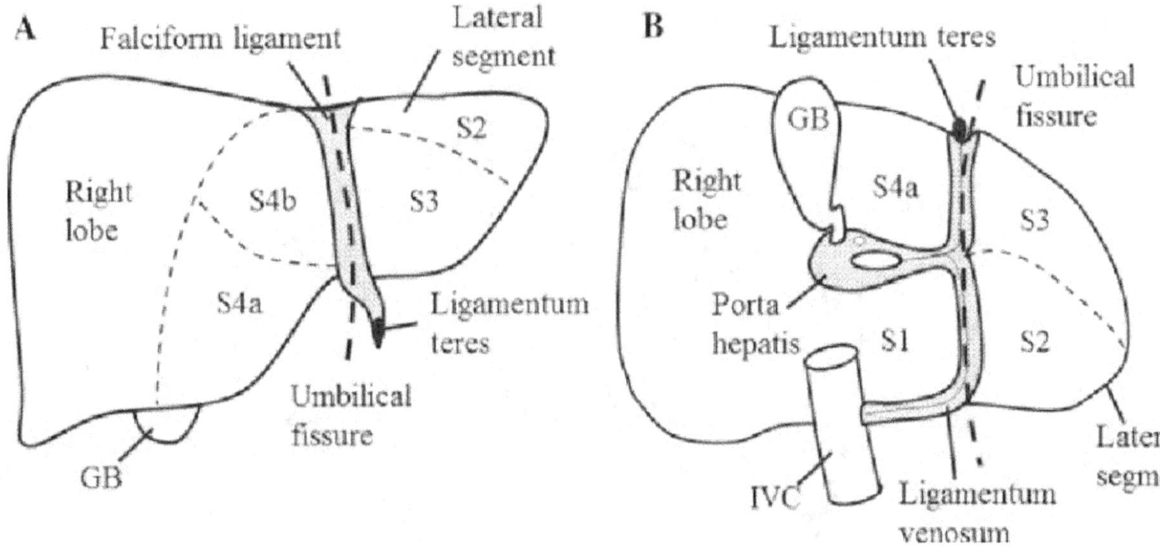
A
Falciform ligament
Lateral segment
S2
Right lobe
S4b
S3
S4a
Ligamentum teres
Umbilical fissure
GB
B
Ligamentum teres
Umbilical fissure
GB
Right lobe
S4a
S3
Porta hepatis
S1
S2
Lateral segment
IVC
Ligamentum venosum

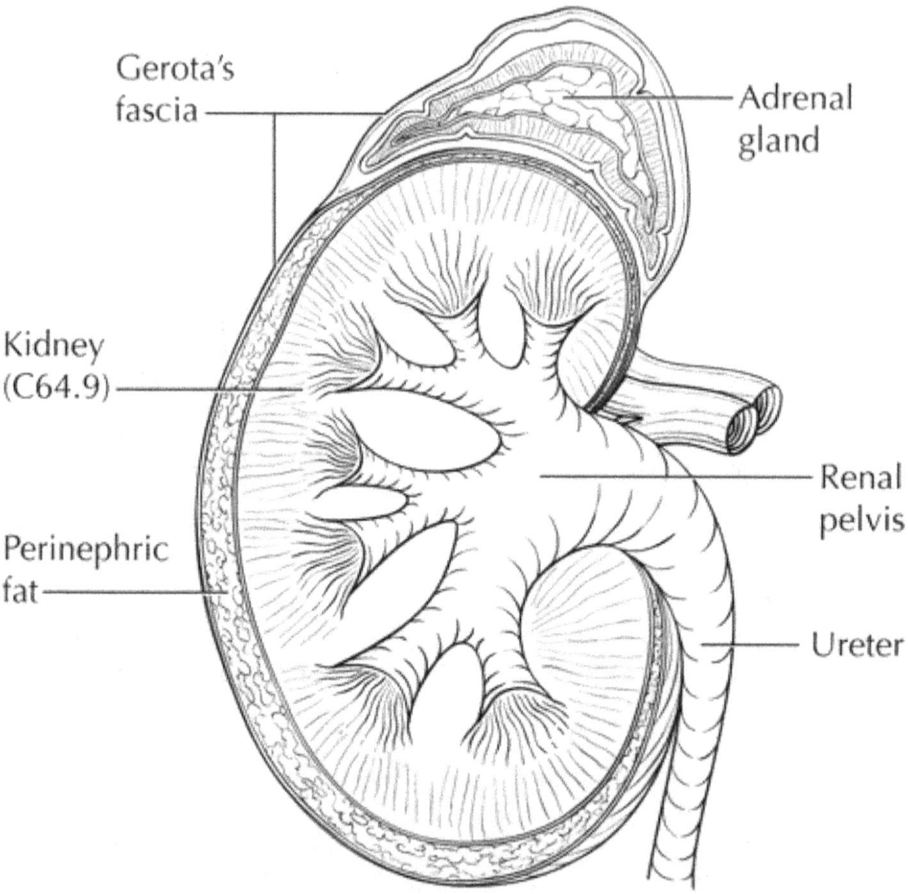
Gerota's
fascia
Adrenal
gland
Kidney
(C64.9)
Renal
pelvis
Perinephric
fat
Ureter

Tooth Diagram

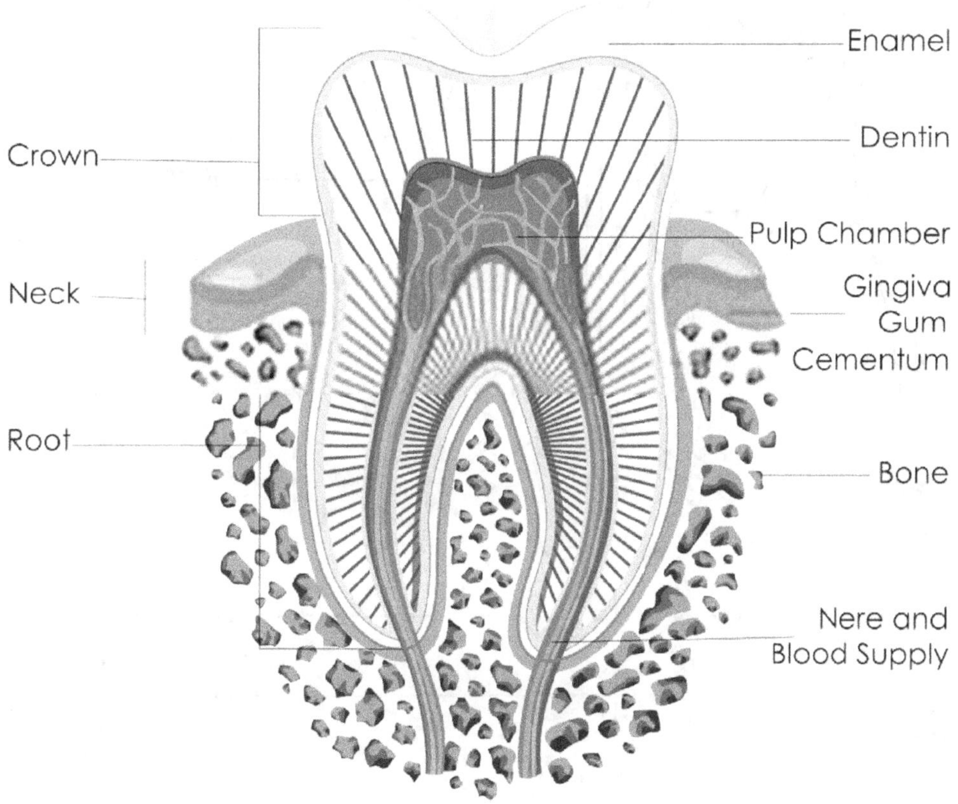

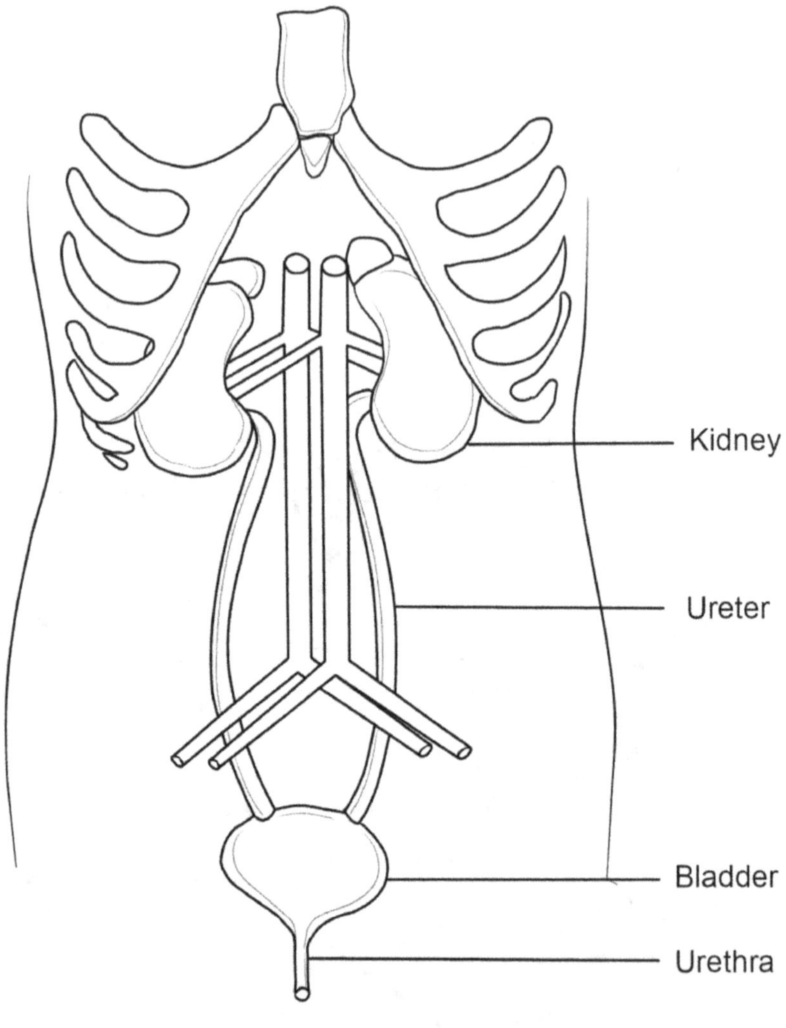

The Urinary System

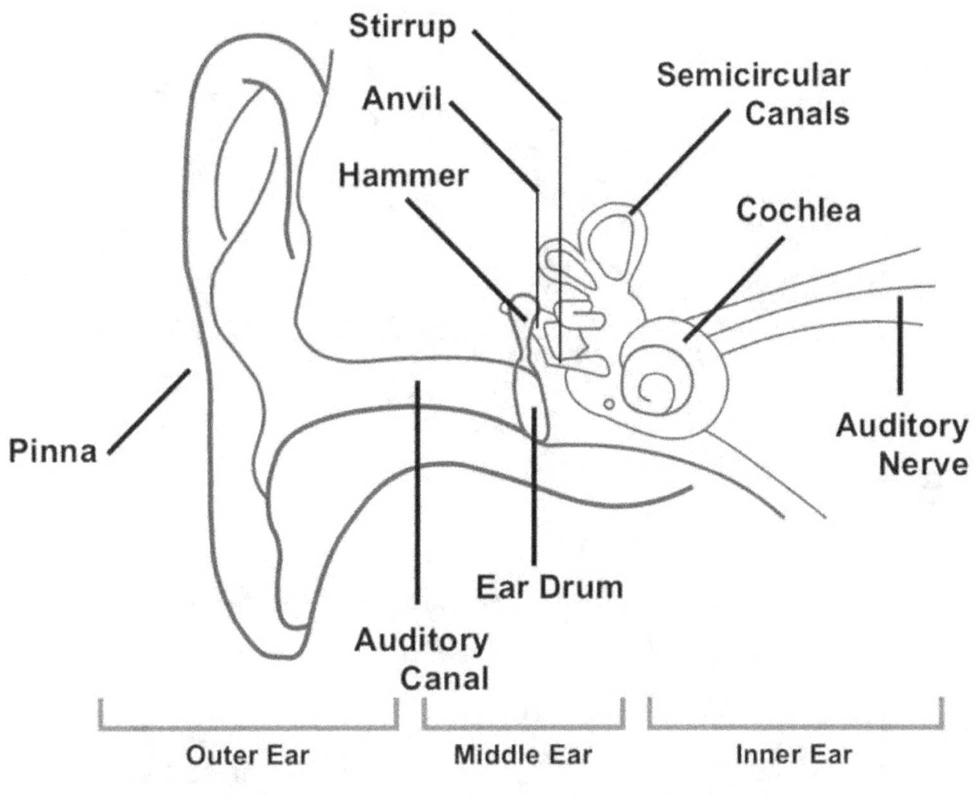
Stirrup
Anvil
Hammer
Semicircular Canals
Cochlea
Auditory Nerve
Pinna
Ear Drum
Auditory Canal
Outer Ear
Middle Ear
Inner Ear

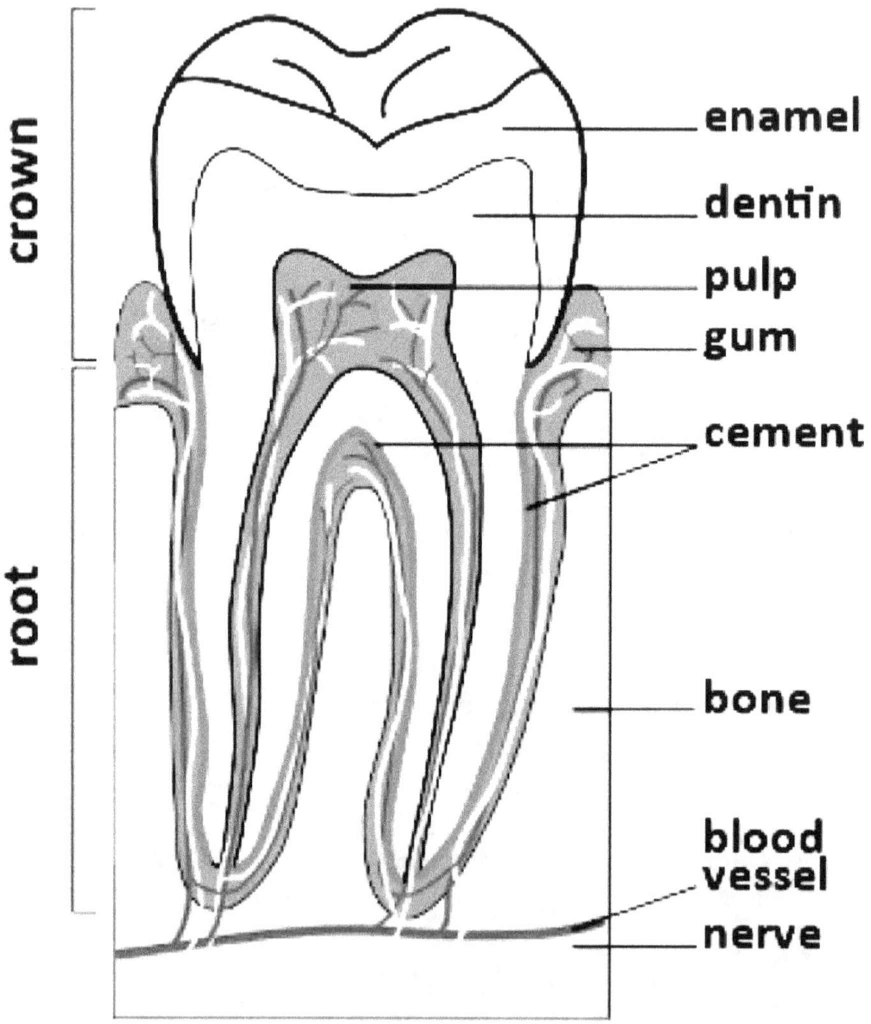
crown
root
enamel
dentin
pulp
gum
cement
bone
blood
vessel
nerve

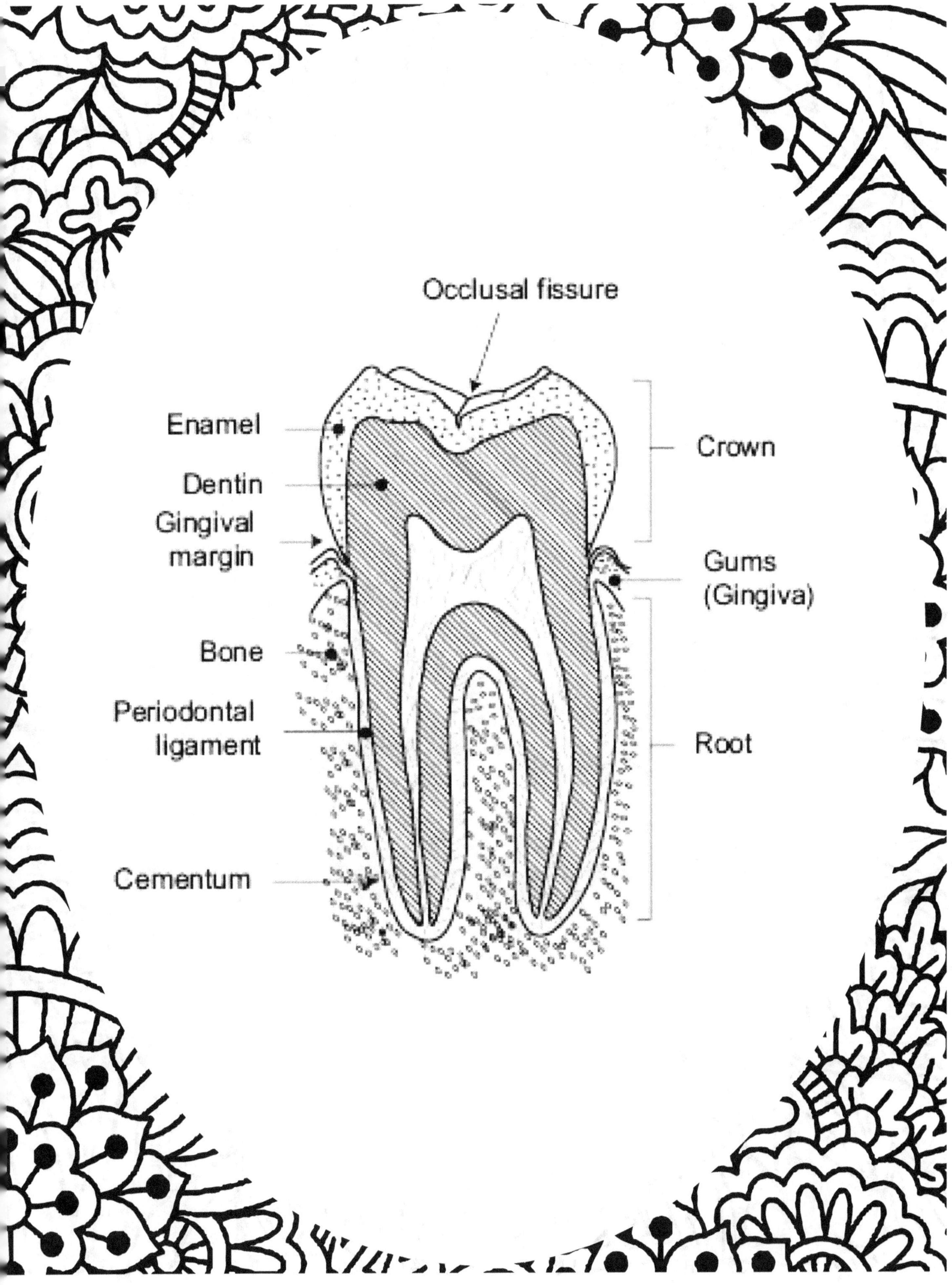
Occlusal fissure
Enamel
Dentin
Gingival margin
Bone
Periodontal ligament
Cementum
Crown
Gums (Gingiva)
Root

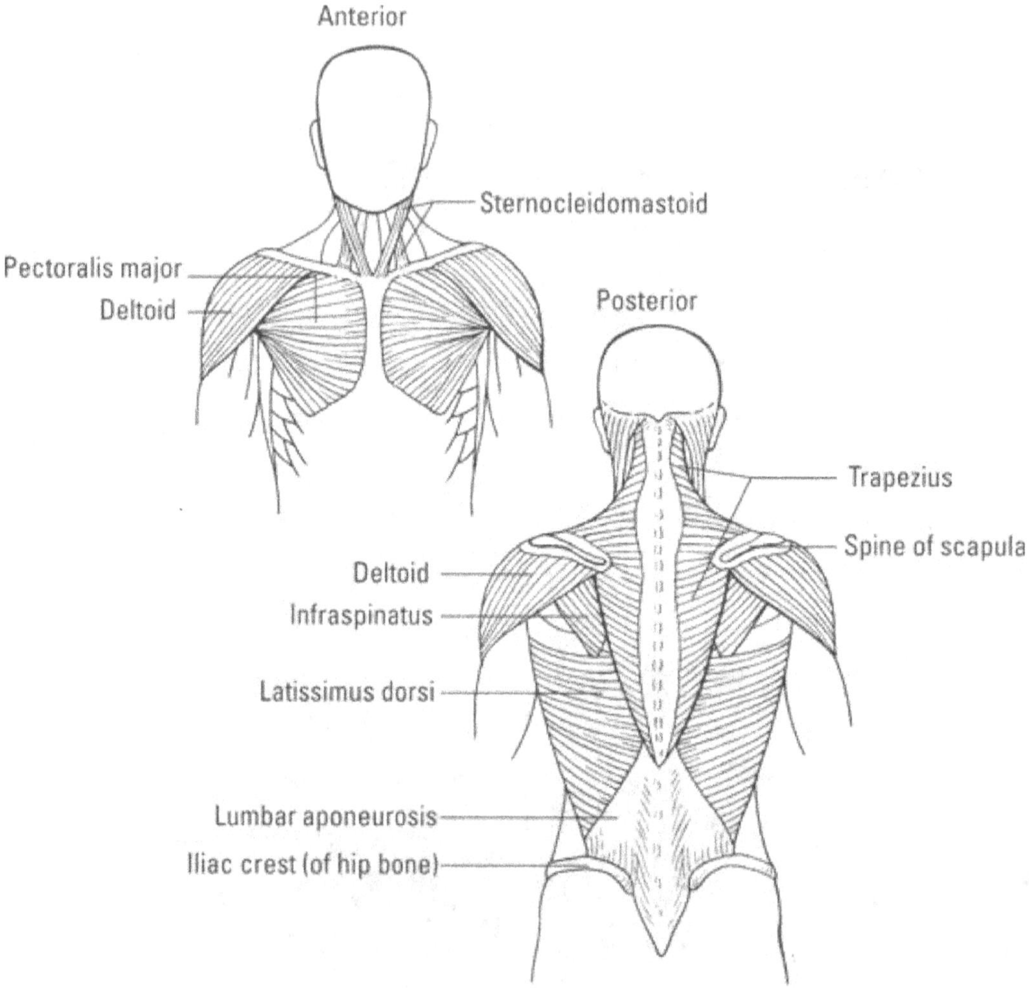
Anterior
Sternocleidomastoid
Pectoralis major
Deltoid
Posterior
Trapezius
Spine of scapula
Deltoid
Infraspinatus
Latissimus dorsi
Lumbar aponeurosis
Iliac crest (of hip bone)

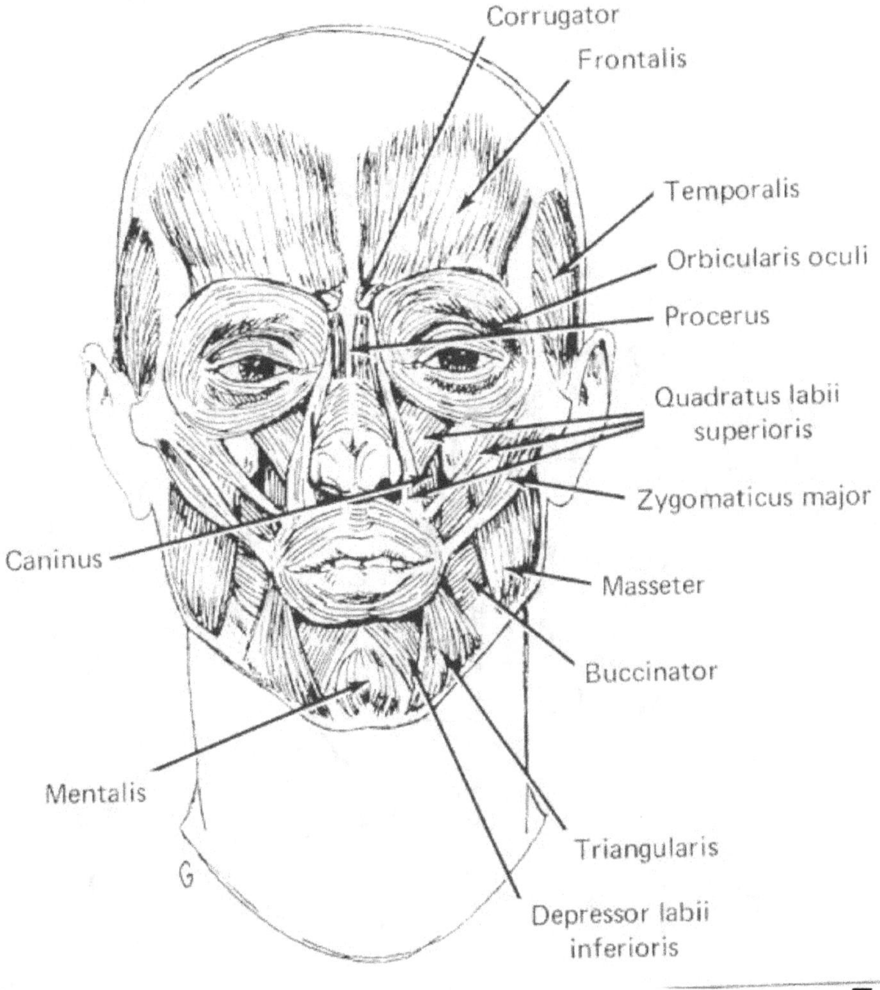
Corrugator
Frontalis
Temporalis
Orbicularis oculi
Procerus
Quadratus labii superioris
Zygomaticus major
Caninus
Masseter
Buccinator
Mentalis
Triangularis
Depressor labii inferioris

Female Reproductive Organs

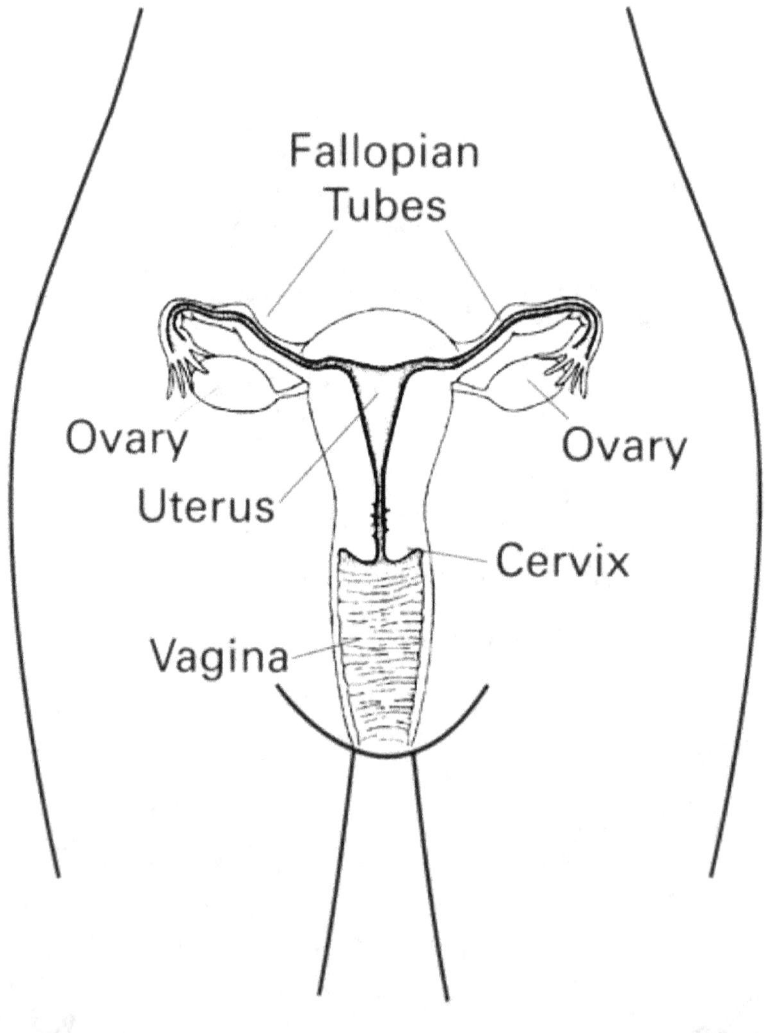

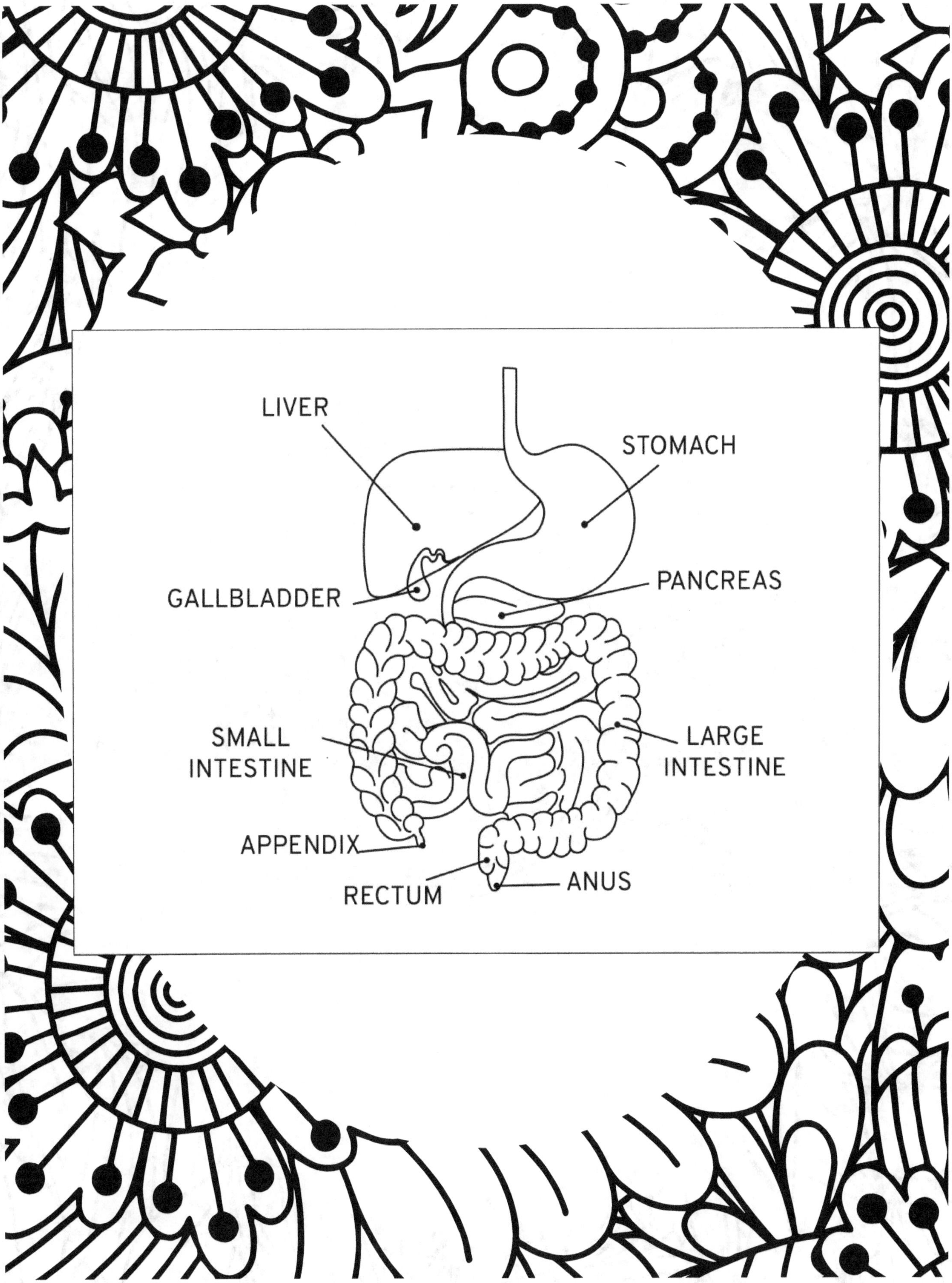
LIVER
STOMACH
GALLBLADDER
PANCREAS
SMALL INTESTINE
LARGE INTESTINE
APPENDIX
RECTUM
ANUS

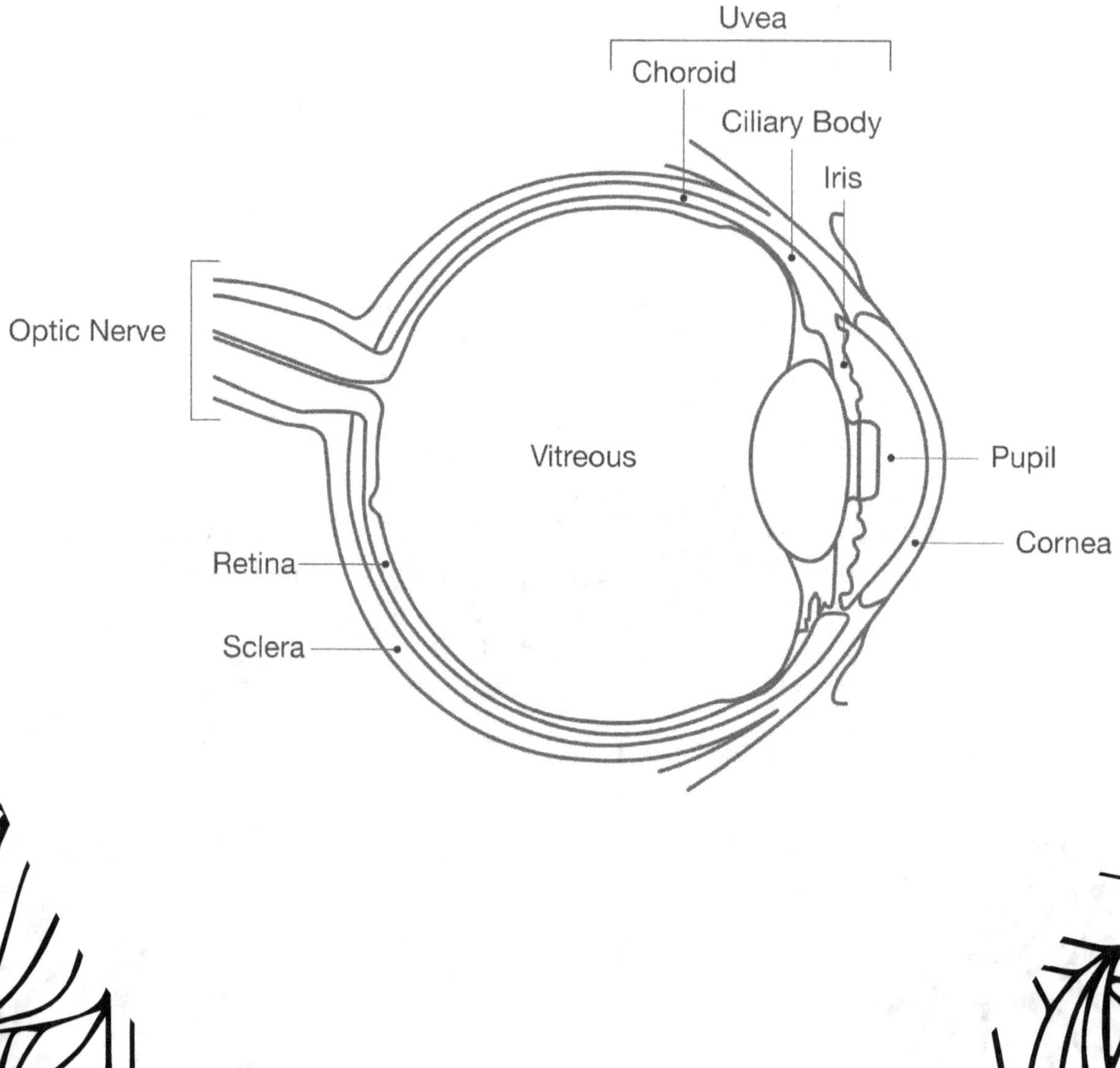

Uvea
Choroid
Ciliary Body
Iris
Optic Nerve
Vitreous
Pupil
Cornea
Retina
Sclera

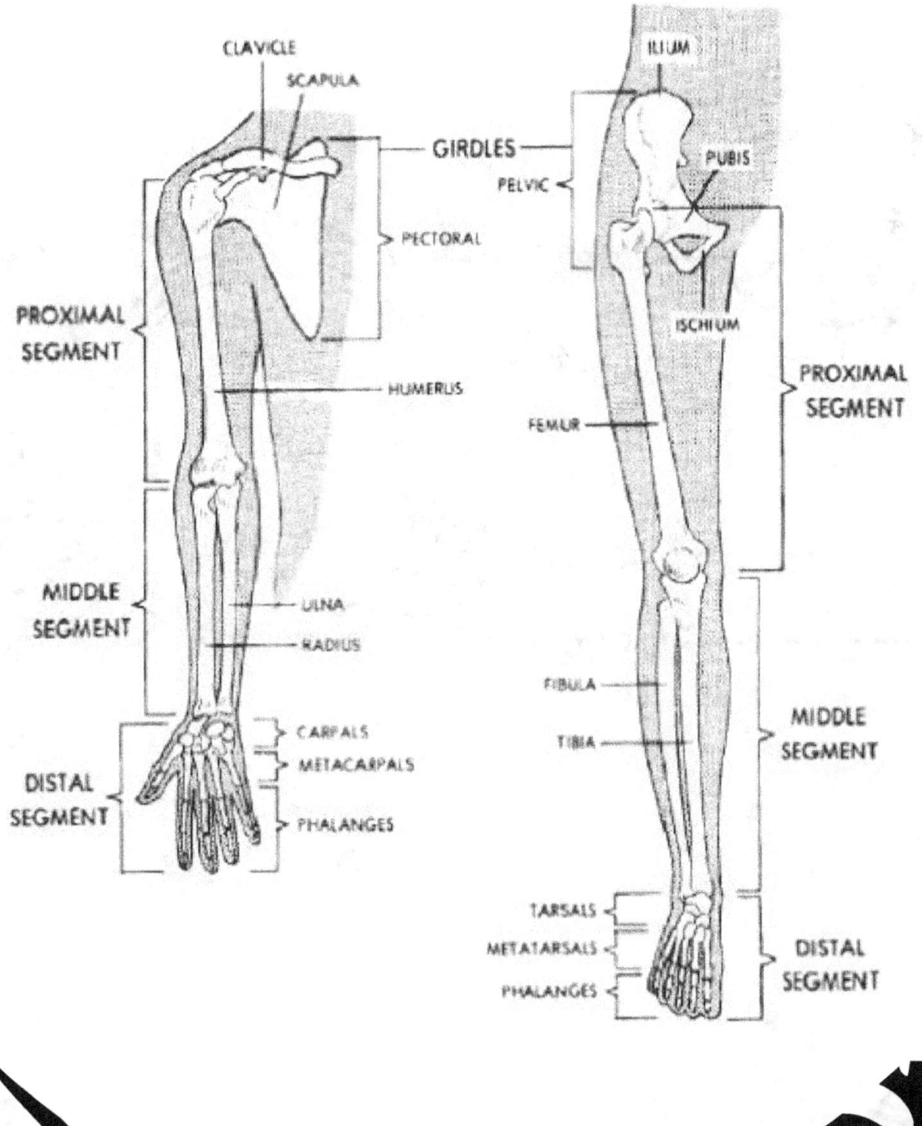
CLAVICLE
SCAPULA
GIRDLES
PELVIC
PECTORAL
ILIUM
PUBIS
ISCHIUM
PROXIMAL SEGMENT
HUMERUS
FEMUR
PROXIMAL SEGMENT
MIDDLE SEGMENT
ULNA
RADIUS
FIBULA
TIBIA
MIDDLE SEGMENT
CARPALS
METACARPALS
DISTAL SEGMENT
PHALANGES
TARSALS
METATARSALS
PHALANGES
DISTAL SEGMENT

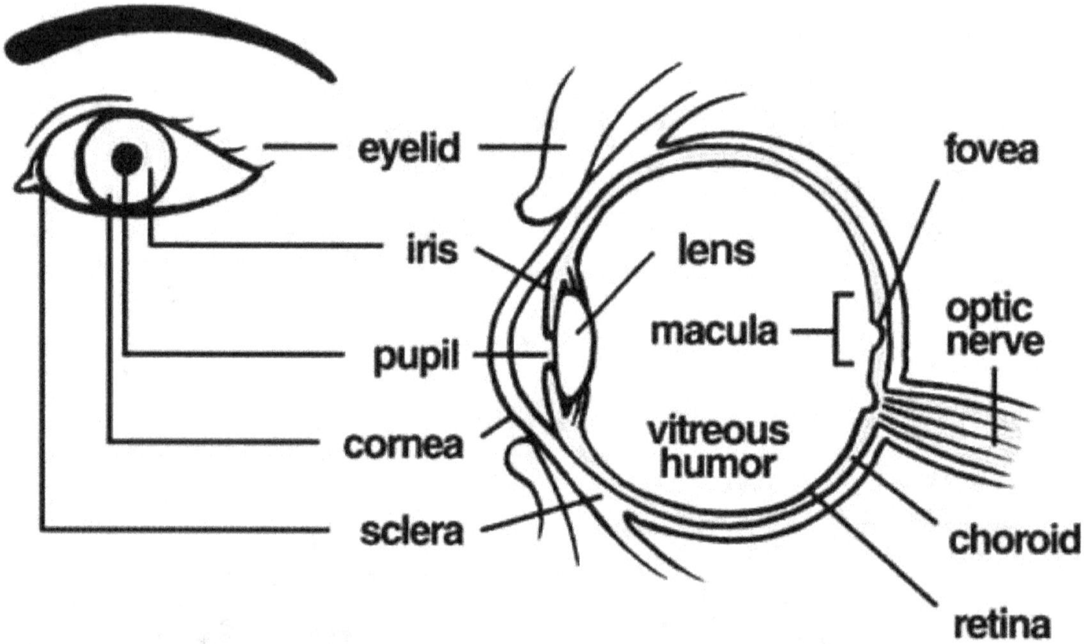
eyelid
iris
pupil
cornea
sclera
lens
macula
vitreous humor
fovea
optic nerve
choroid
retina

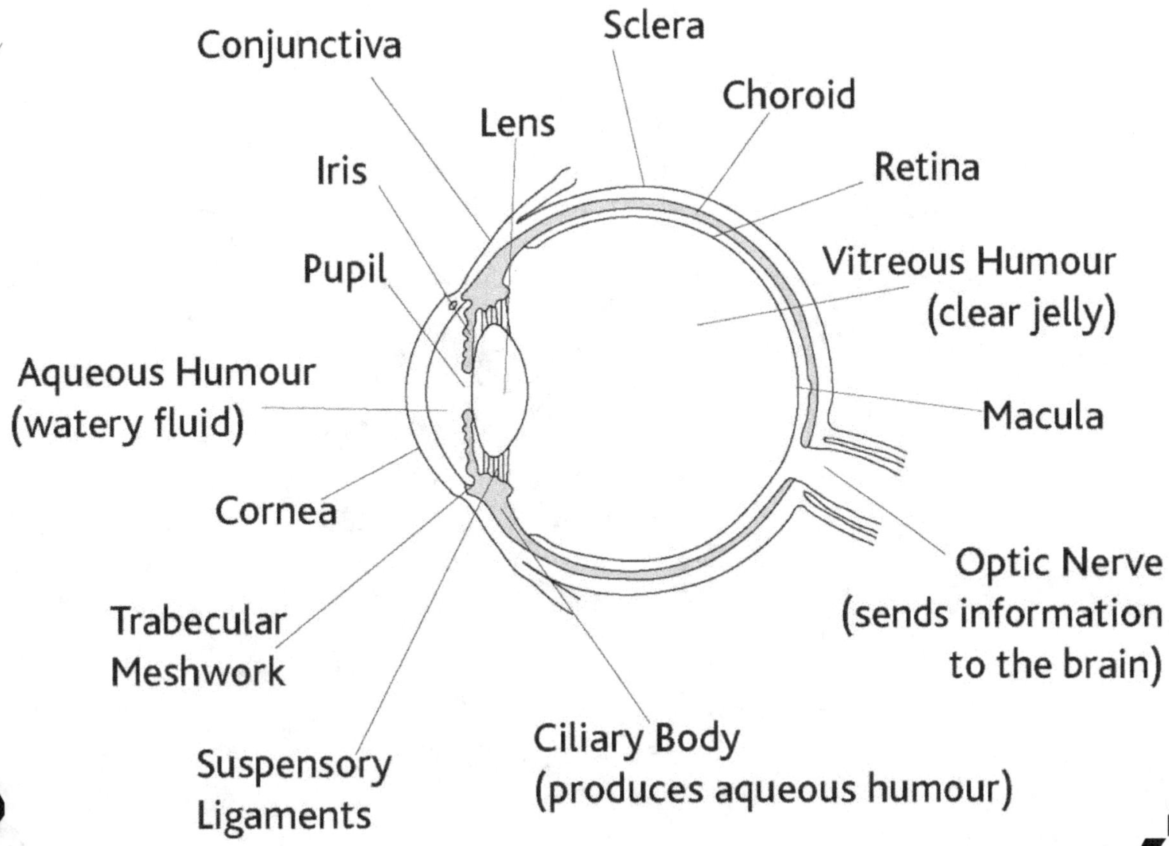
Conjunctiva
Sclera
Choroid
Lens
Iris
Retina
Pupil
Vitreous Humour
(clear jelly)
Aqueous Humour
(watery fluid)
Macula
Cornea
Optic Nerve
(sends information
to the brain)
Trabecular
Meshwork
Ciliary Body
(produces aqueous humour)
Suspensory
Ligaments

parts of an ear

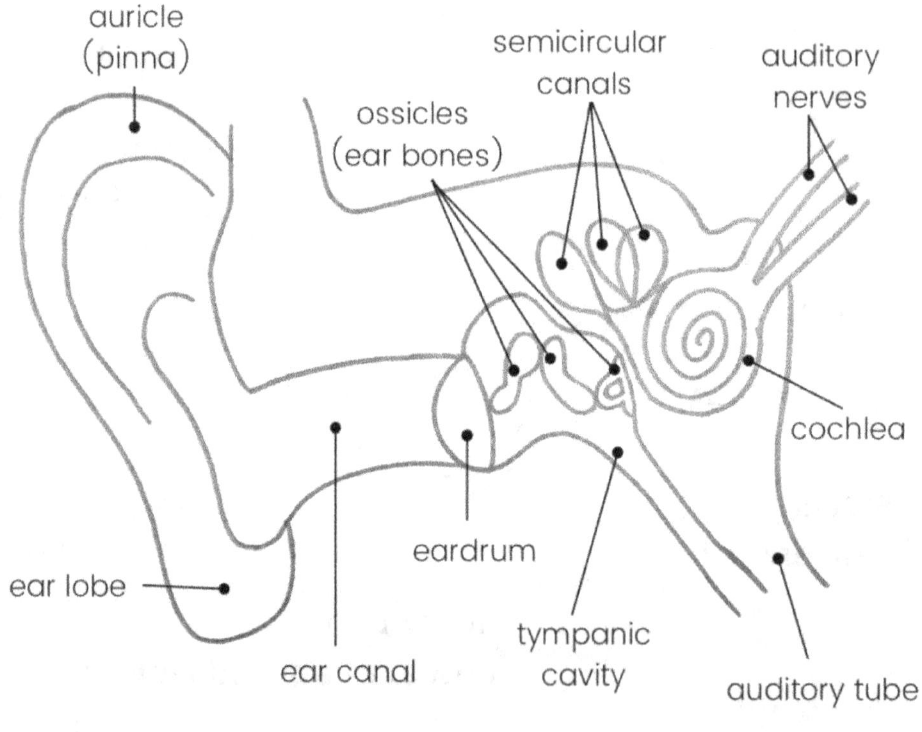

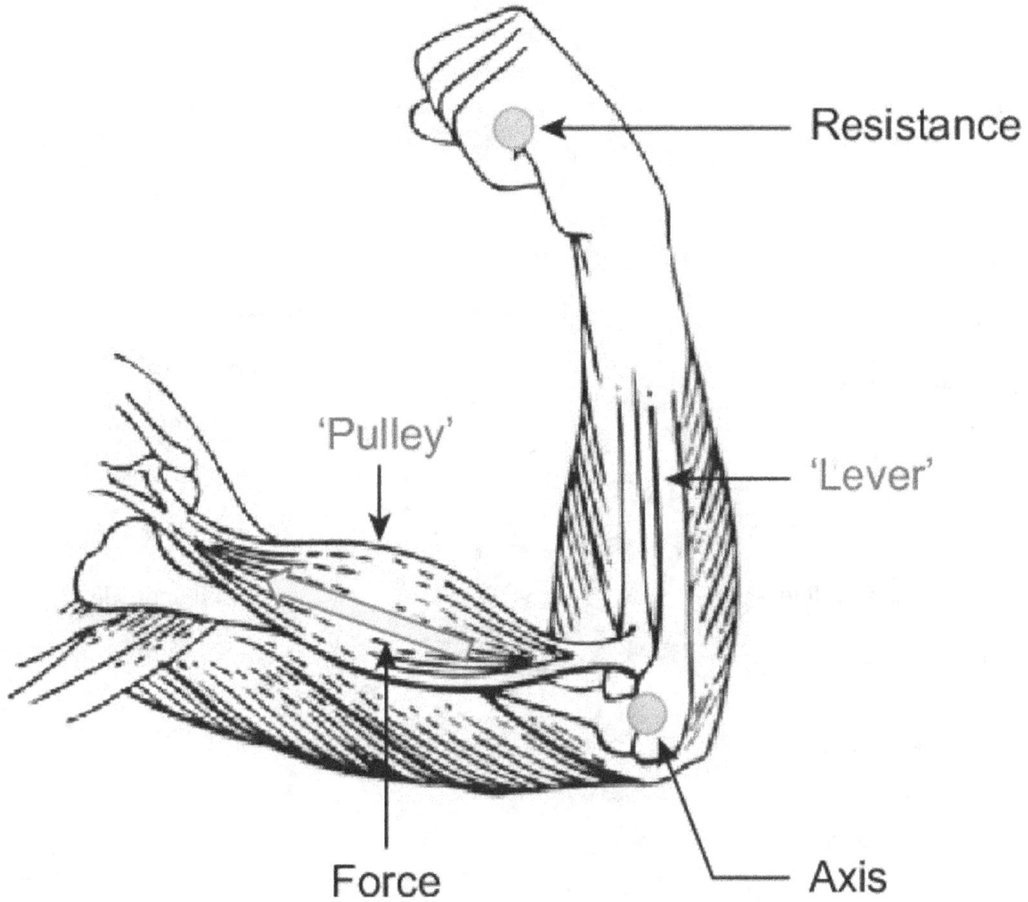
Resistance
'Pulley'
'Lever'
Force
Axis

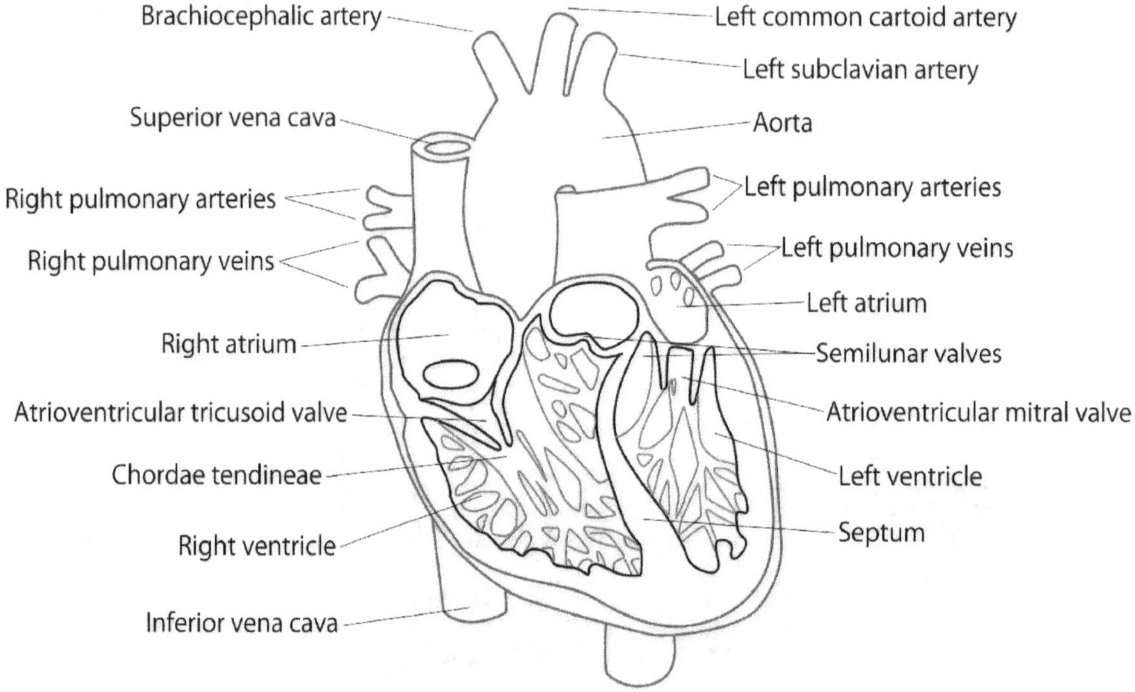
Brachiocephalic artery
Left common cartoid artery
Left subclavian artery
Superior vena cava
Aorta
Right pulmonary arteries
Left pulmonary arteries
Right pulmonary veins
Left pulmonary veins
Left atrium
Right atrium
Semilunar valves
Atrioventricular tricusoid valve
Atrioventricular mitral valve
Chordae tendineae
Left ventricle
Septum
Right ventricle
Inferior vena cava

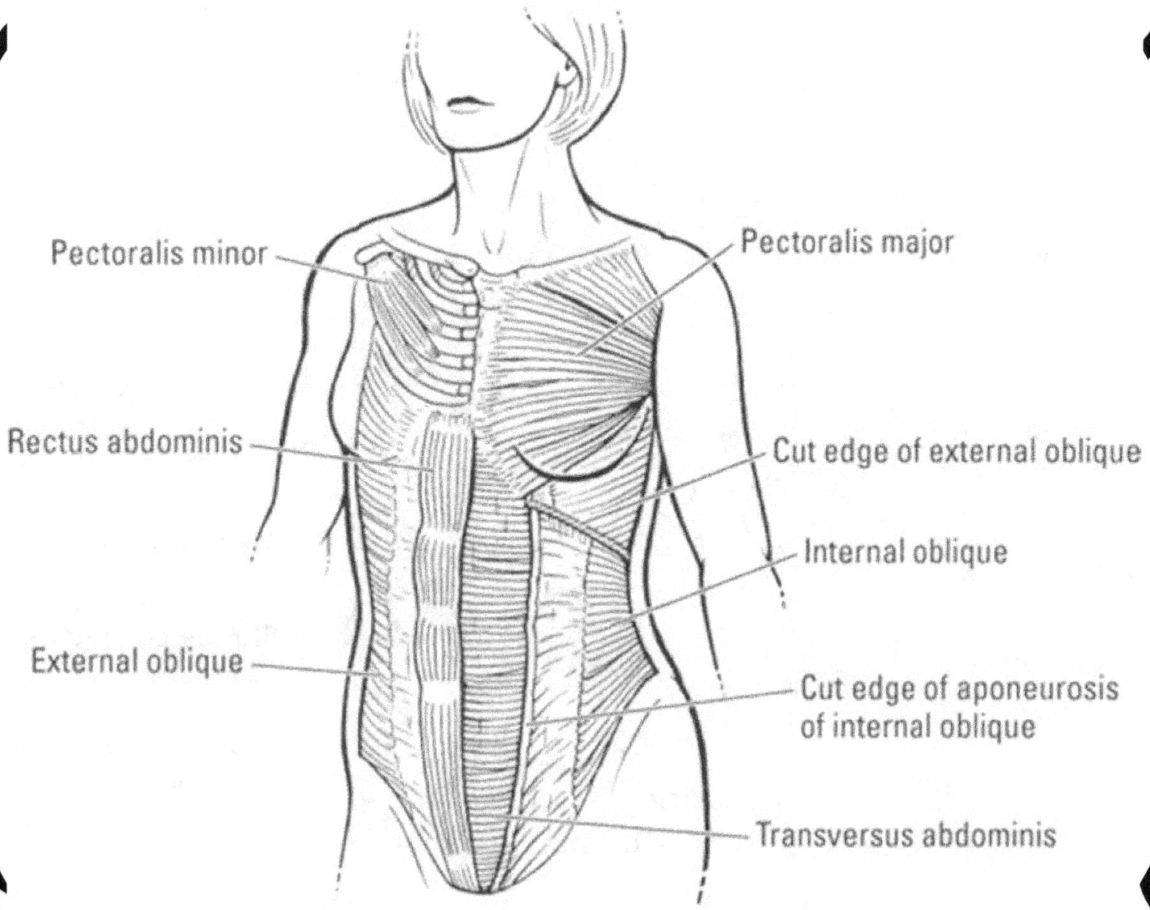
Pectoralis minor
Pectoralis major
Rectus abdominis
Cut edge of external oblique
Internal oblique
External oblique
Cut edge of aponeurosis of internal oblique
Transversus abdominis

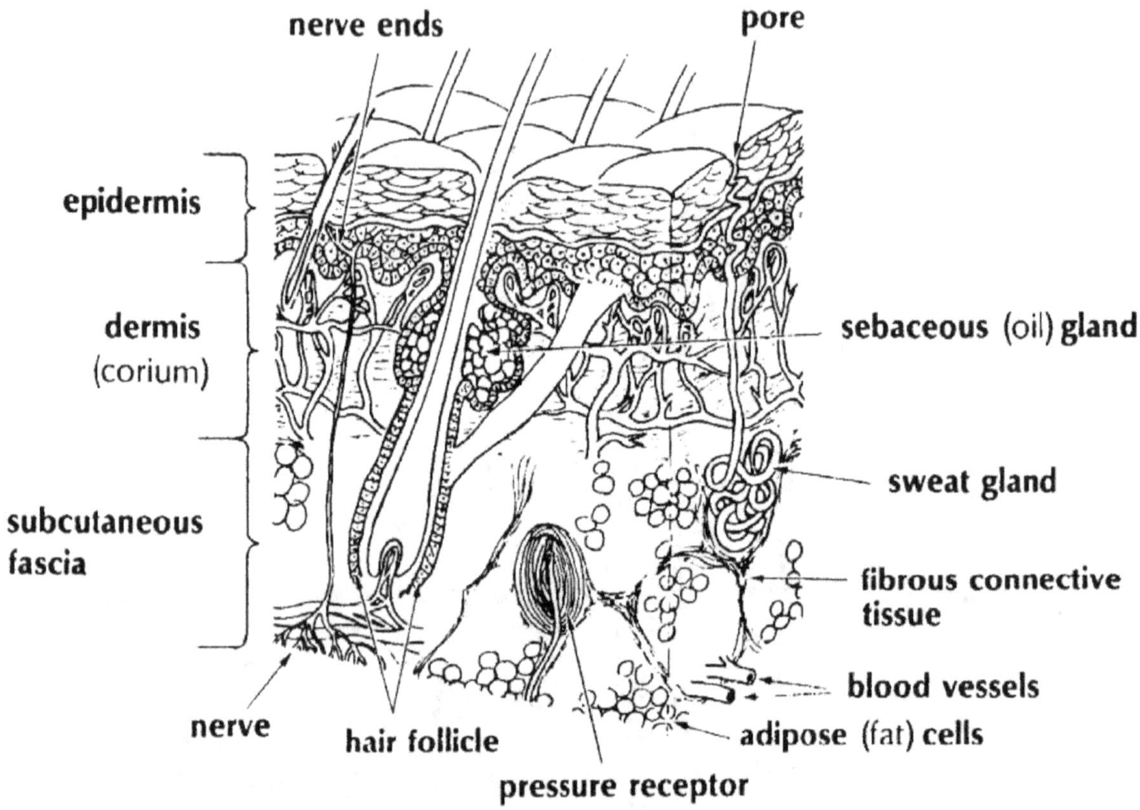
nerve ends
pore
epidermis
dermis
(corium)
sebaceous (oil) gland
sweat gland
subcutaneous
fascia
fibrous connective
tissue
blood vessels
nerve
hair follicle
adipose (fat) cells
pressure receptor

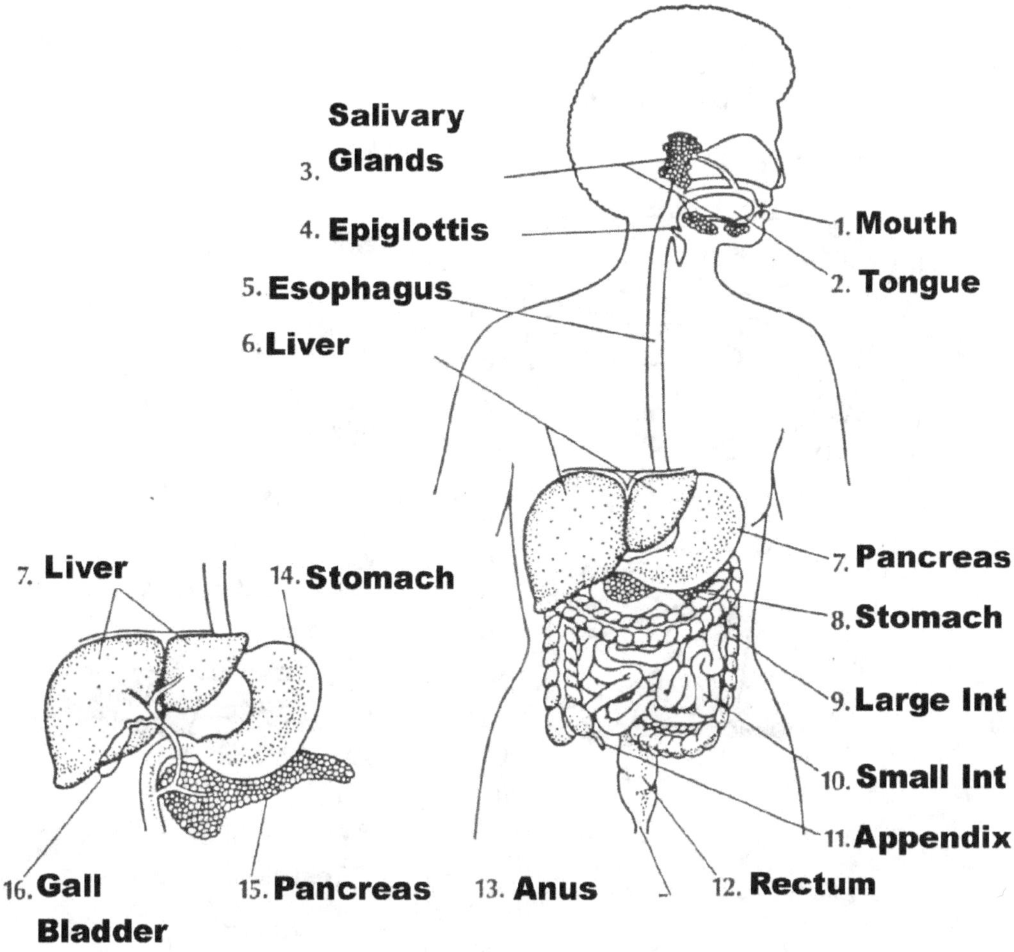
Salivary
3. Glands
4. Epiglottis
5. Esophagus
6. Liver
1. Mouth
2. Tongue
7. Pancreas
8. Stomach
9. Large Int
10. Small Int
11. Appendix
12. Rectum
13. Anus
7. Liver
14. Stomach
15. Pancreas
16. Gall
Bladder

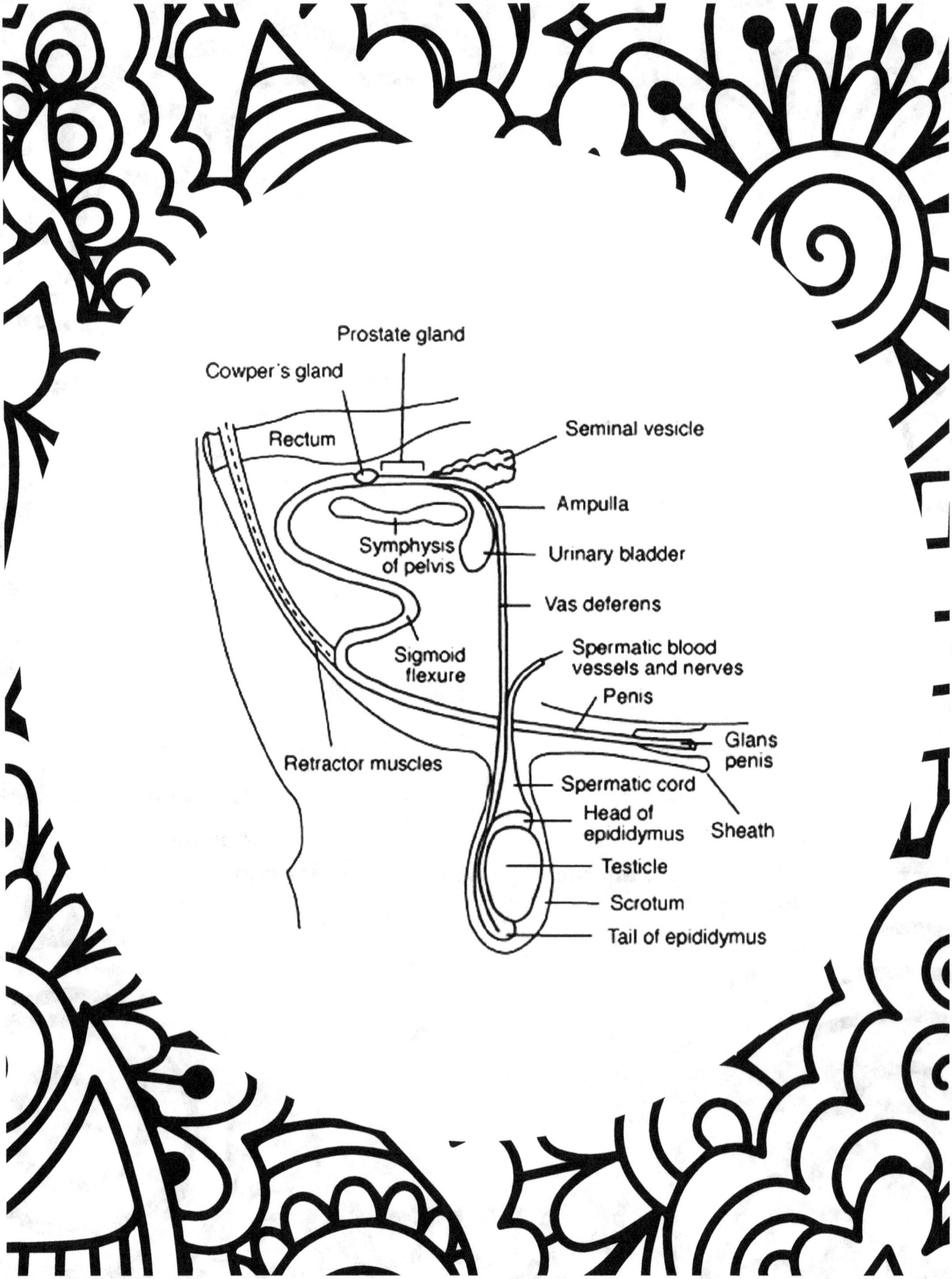
Prostate gland
Cowper's gland
Rectum
Seminal vesicle
Ampulla
Symphysis of pelvis
Urinary bladder
Vas deferens
Sigmoid flexure
Spermatic blood vessels and nerves
Penis
Glans penis
Retractor muscles
Spermatic cord
Head of epididymus
Sheath
Testicle
Scrotum
Tail of epididymus

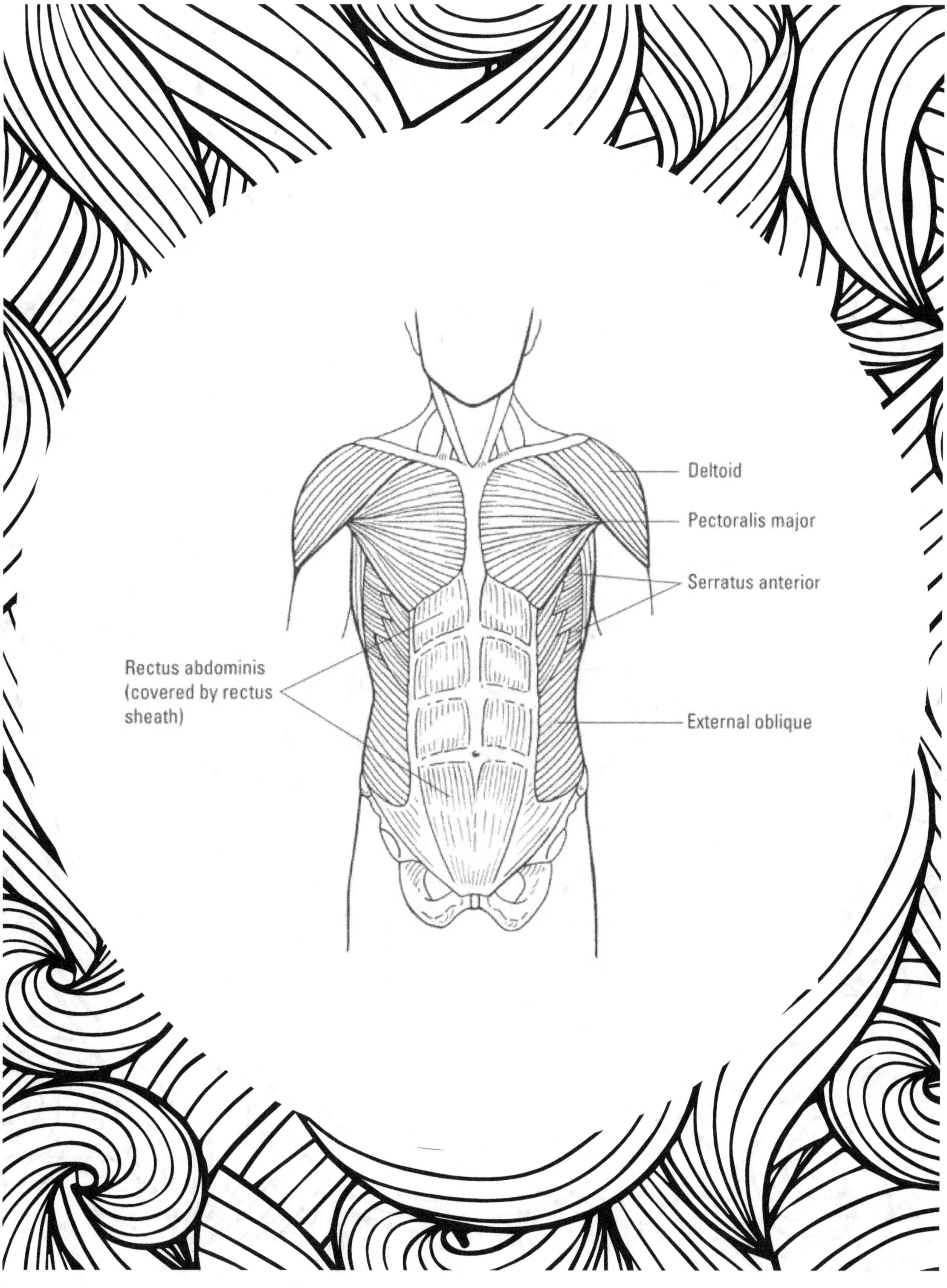
Deltoid
Pectoralis major
Serratus anterior
Rectus abdominis (covered by rectus sheath)
External oblique

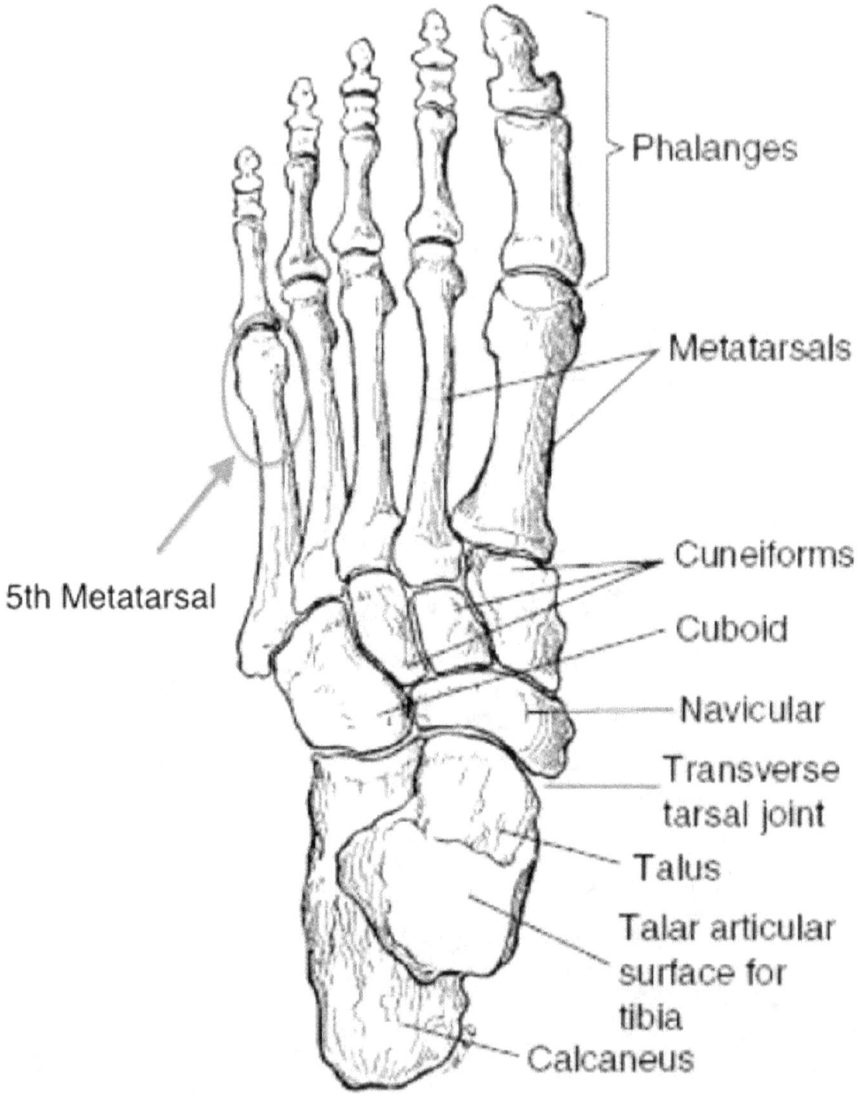
Phalanges
Metatarsals
Cuneiforms
5th Metatarsal
Cuboid
Navicular
Transverse tarsal joint
Talus
Talar articular surface for tibia
Calcaneus

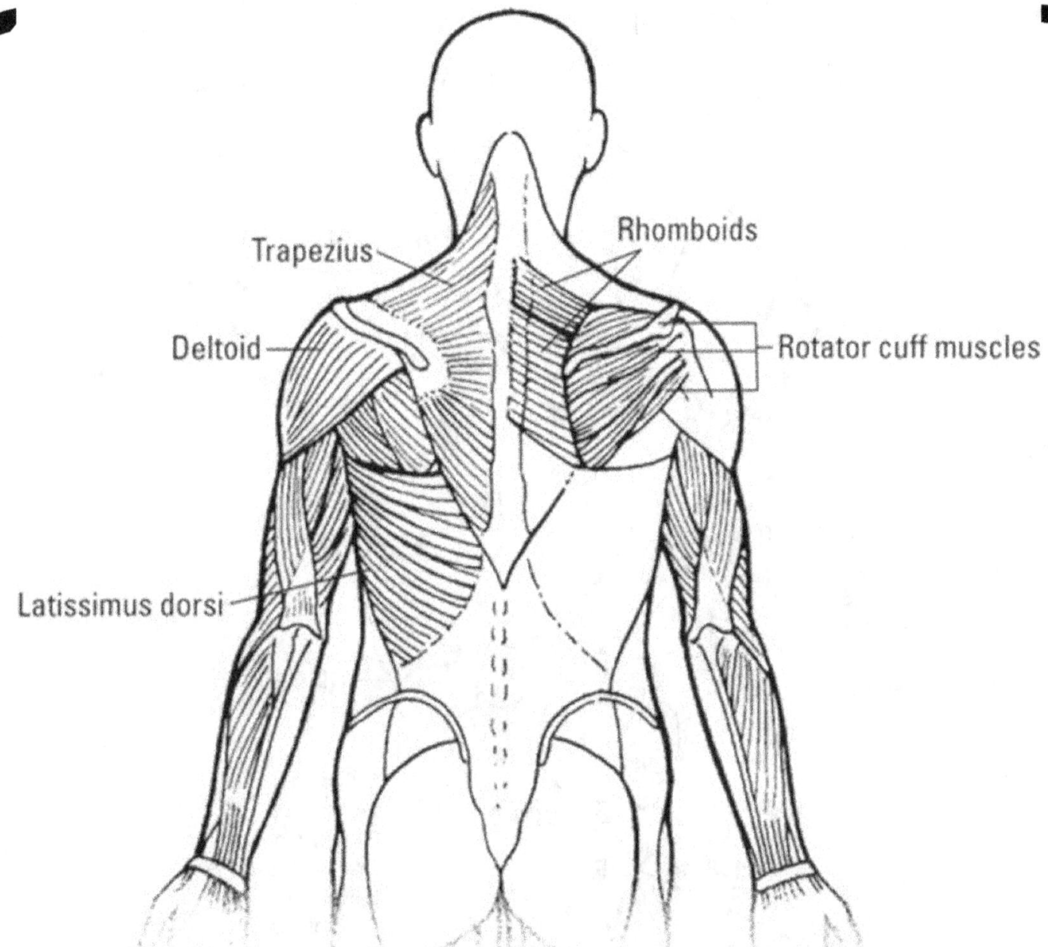
Trapezius
Rhomboids
Deltoid
Rotator cuff muscles
Latissimus dorsi

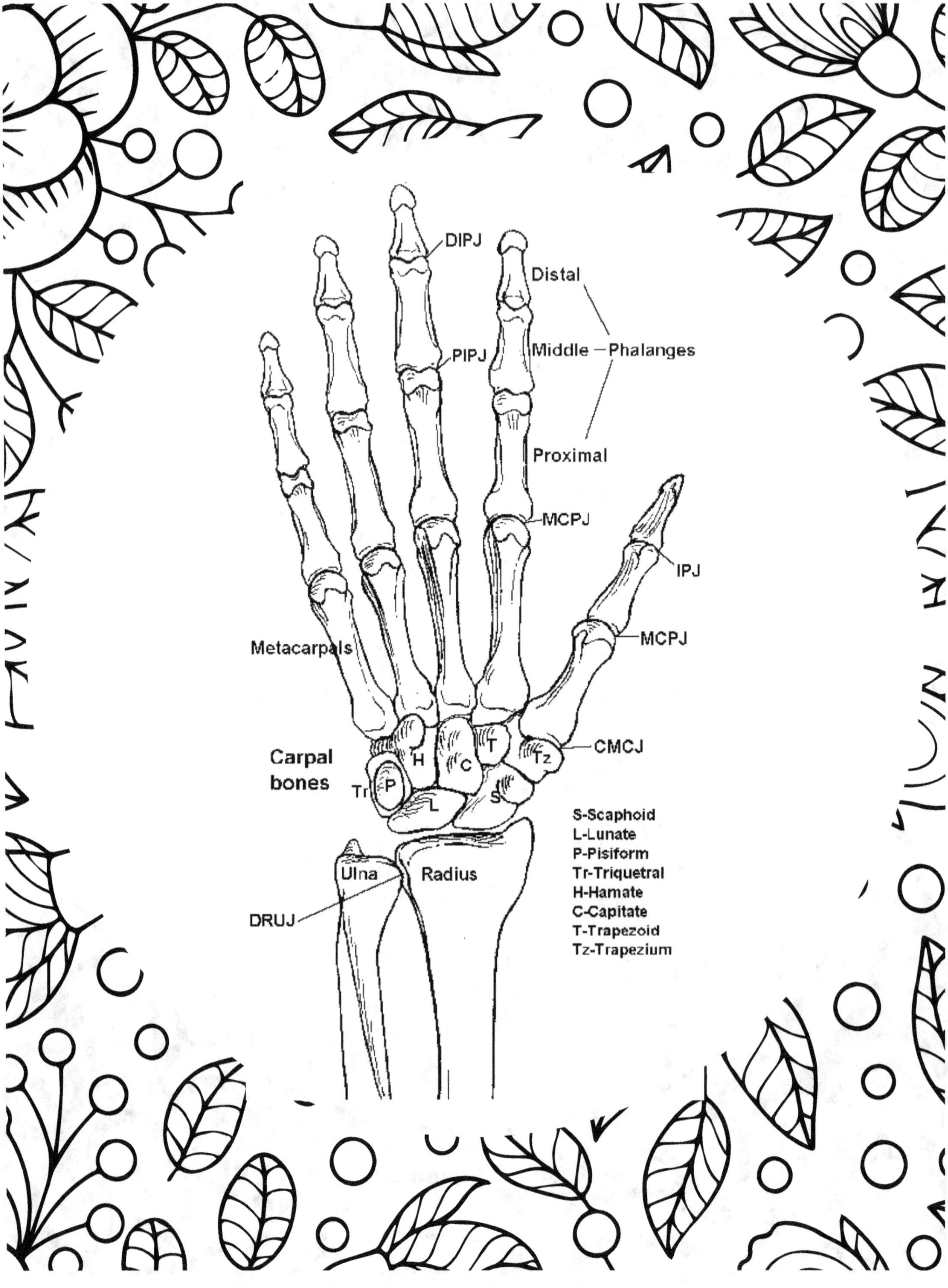
DIPJ
Distal
PIPJ
Middle
Phalanges
Proximal
MCPJ
IPJ
MCPJ
Metacarpals
Carpal bones
H
C
T
Tz
CMCJ
Tr
P
L
S
S-Scaphoid
L-Lunate
P-Pisiform
Tr-Triquetral
H-Hamate
C-Capitate
T-Trapezoid
Tz-Trapezium
Ulna
Radius
DRUJ

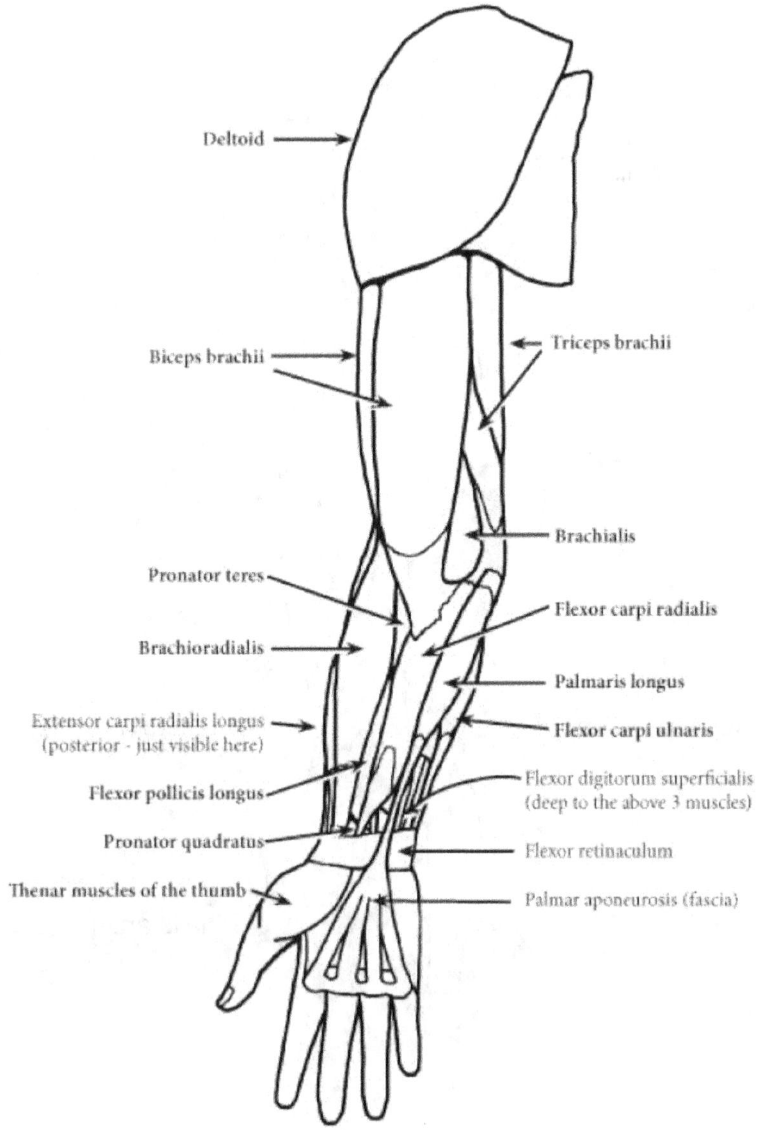
Deltoid
Biceps brachii
Triceps brachii
Brachialis
Pronator teres
Flexor carpi radialis
Brachioradialis
Palmaris longus
Extensor carpi radialis longus
(posterior - just visible here)
Flexor carpi ulnaris
Flexor pollicis longus
Flexor digitorum superficialis
(deep to the above 3 muscles)
Pronator quadratus
Flexor retinaculum
Thenar muscles of the thumb
Palmar aponeurosis (fascia)

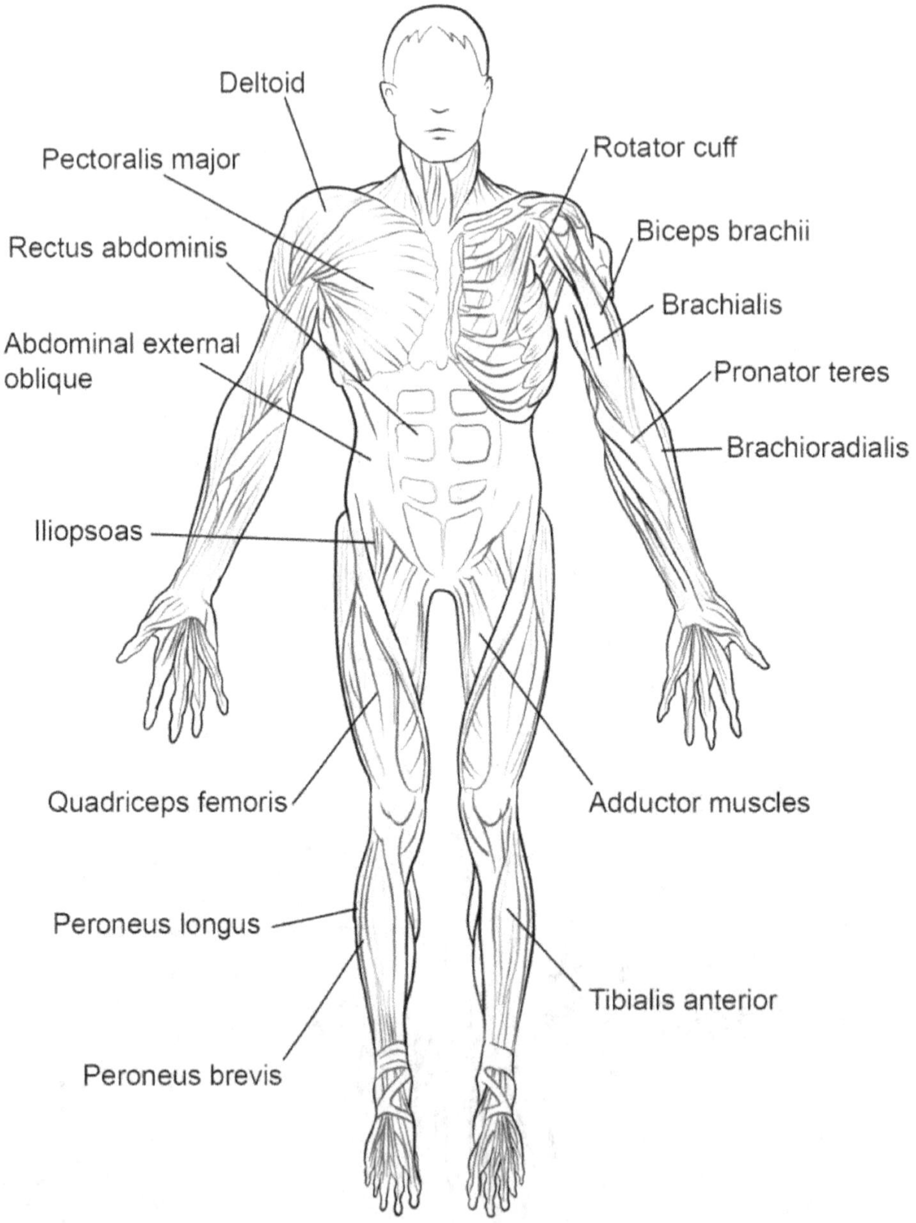

Human Muscles

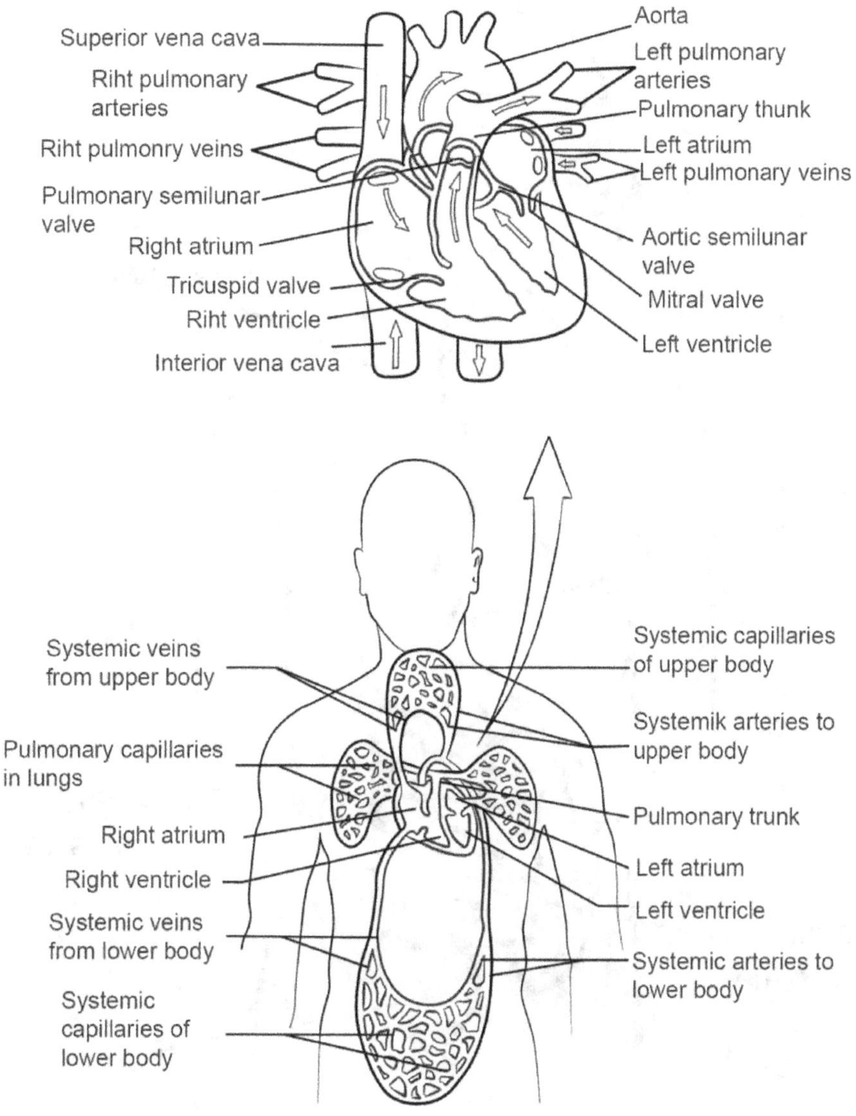

Human Circulatory System

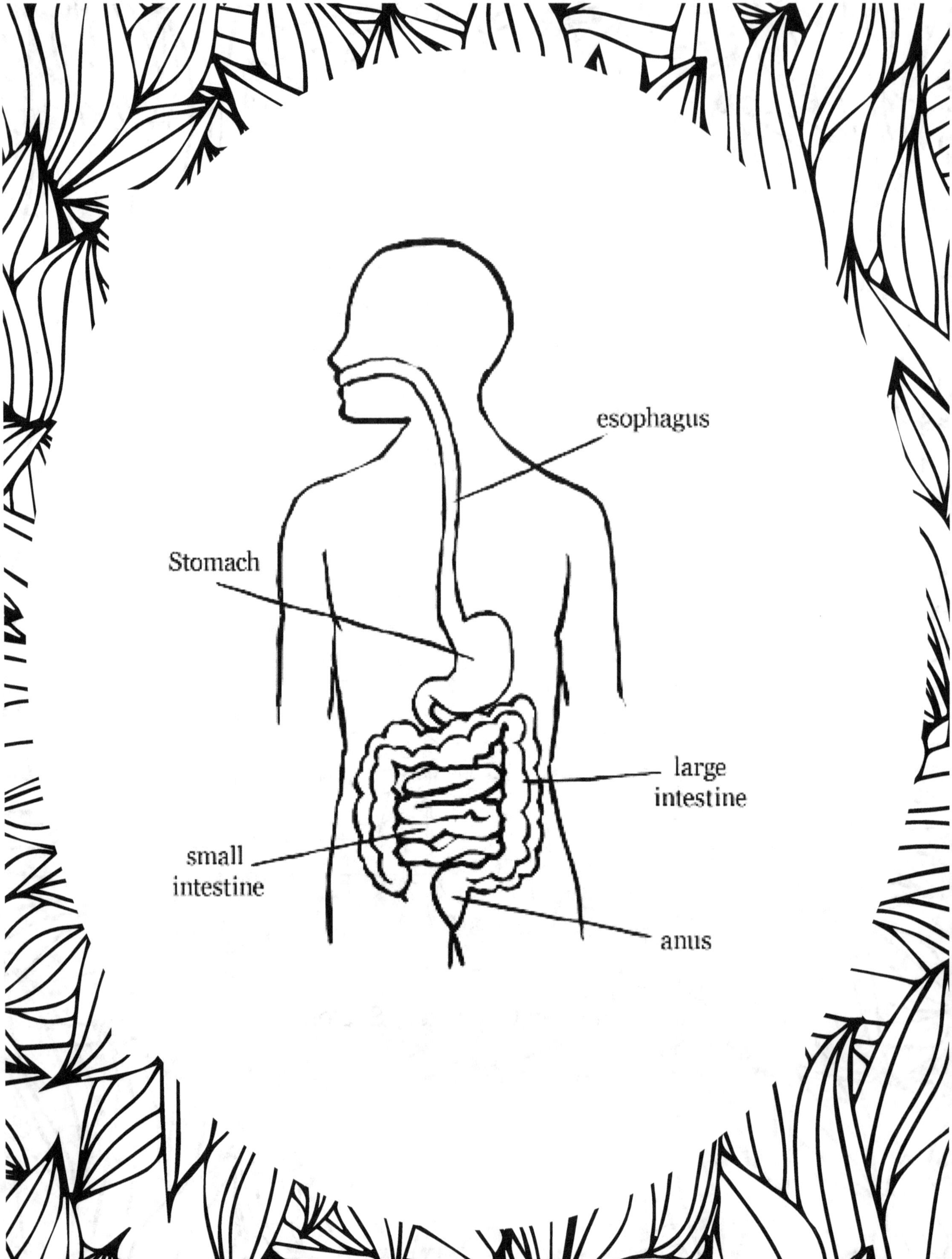
esophagus
Stomach
large
intestine
small
intestine
anus

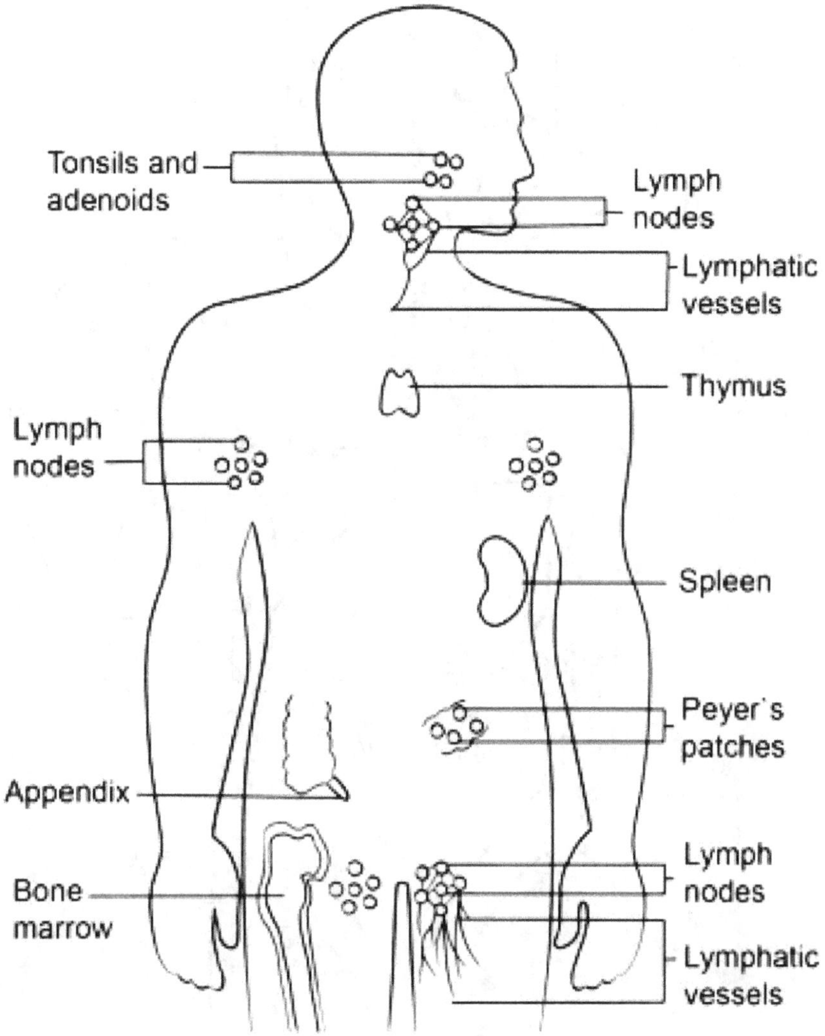

Human Immune System

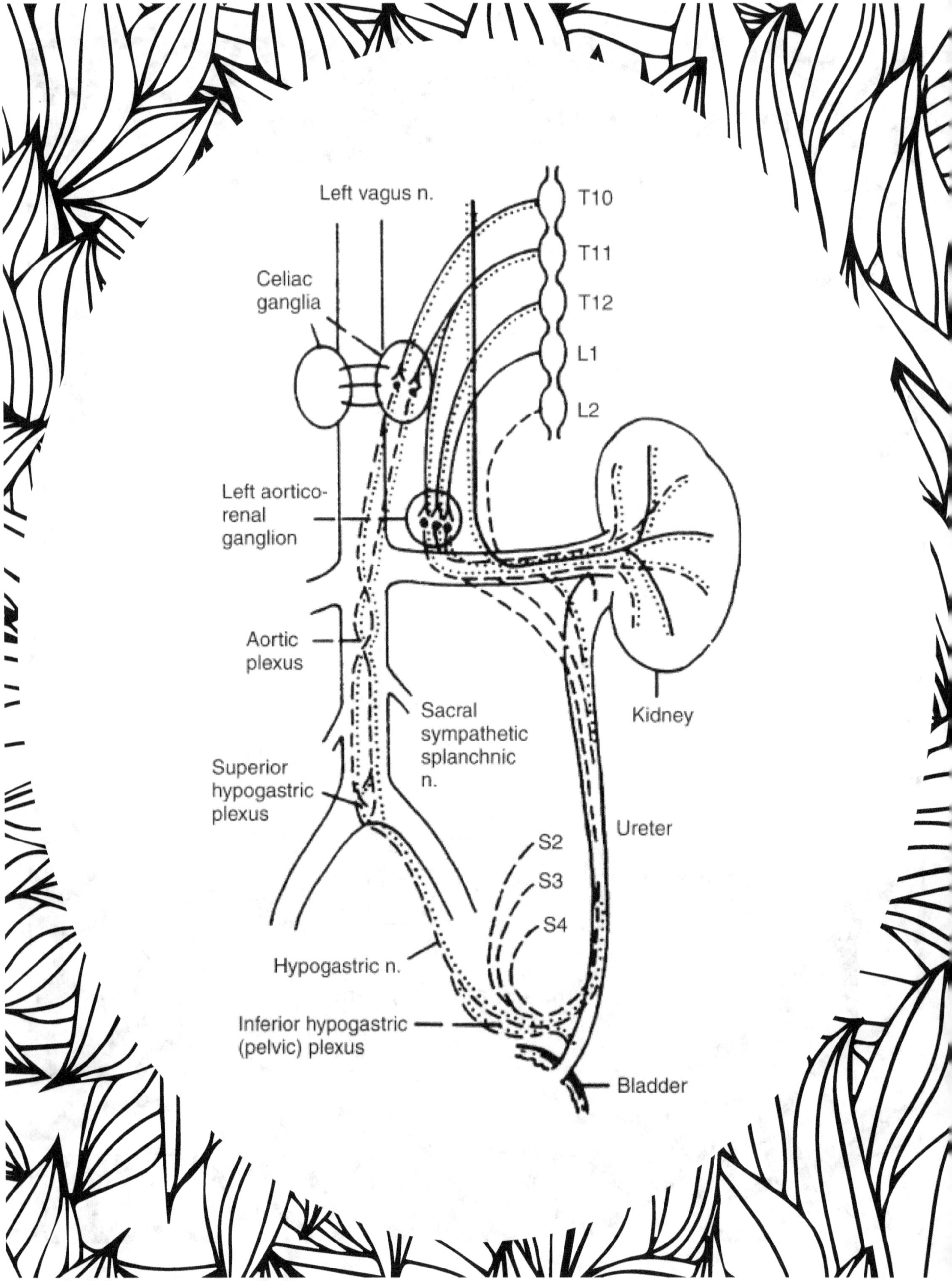
Left vagus n.
T10
T11
T12
L1
L2
Celiac ganglia
Left aortico-renal ganglion
Aortic plexus
Sacral sympathetic splanchnic n.
Kidney
Superior hypogastric plexus
Ureter
S2
S3
S4
Hypogastric n.
Inferior hypogastric (pelvic) plexus
Bladder

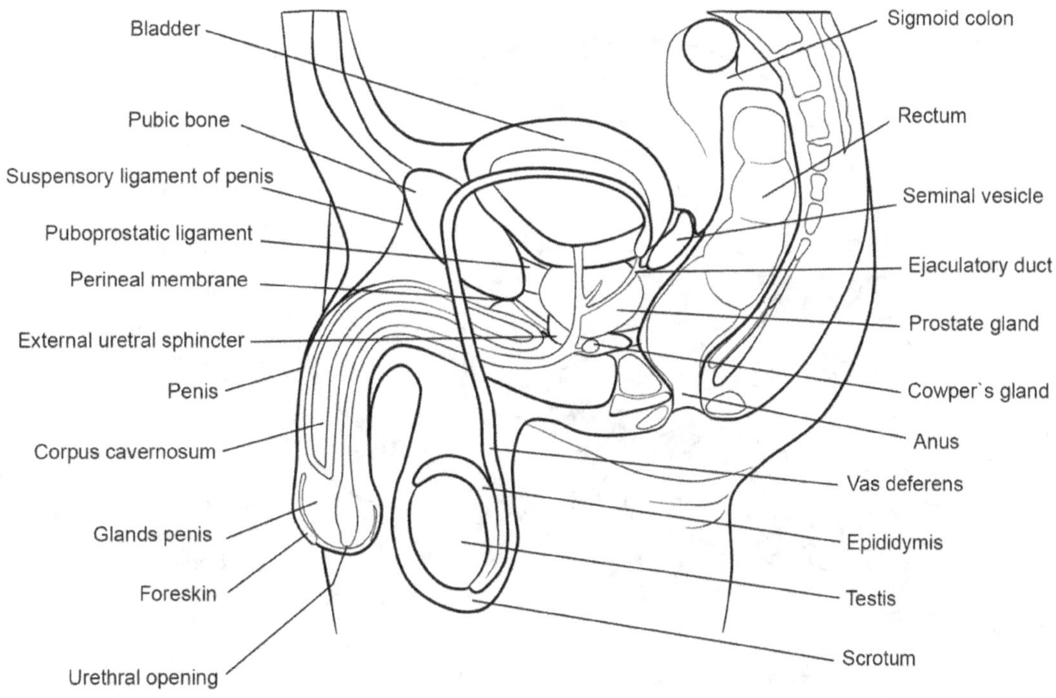

Male reproductive system

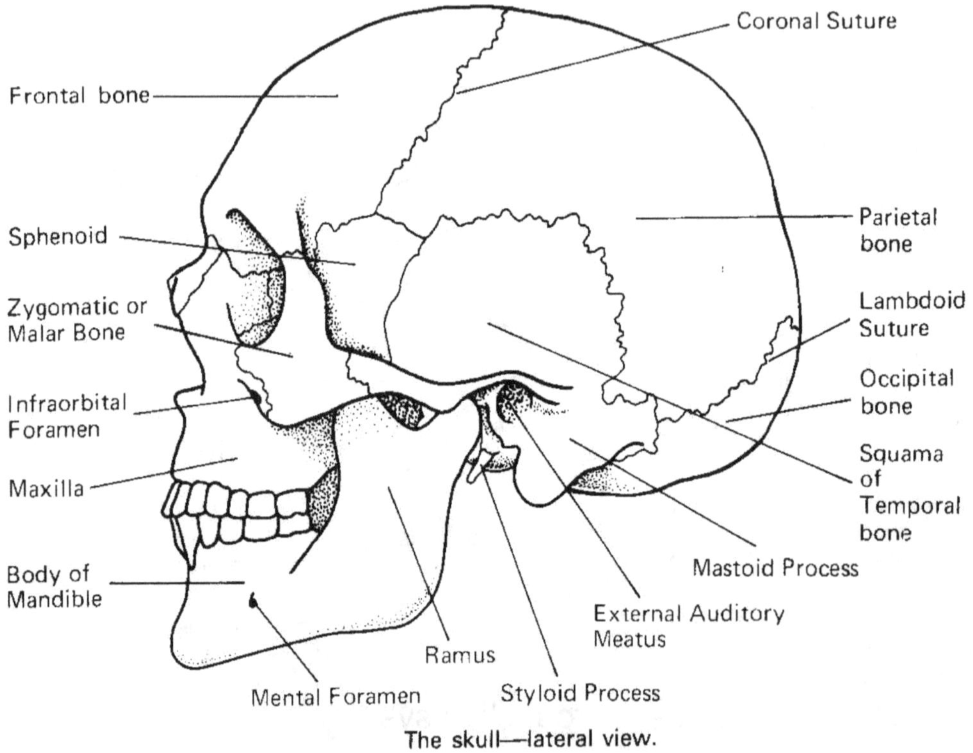

The skull—lateral view.

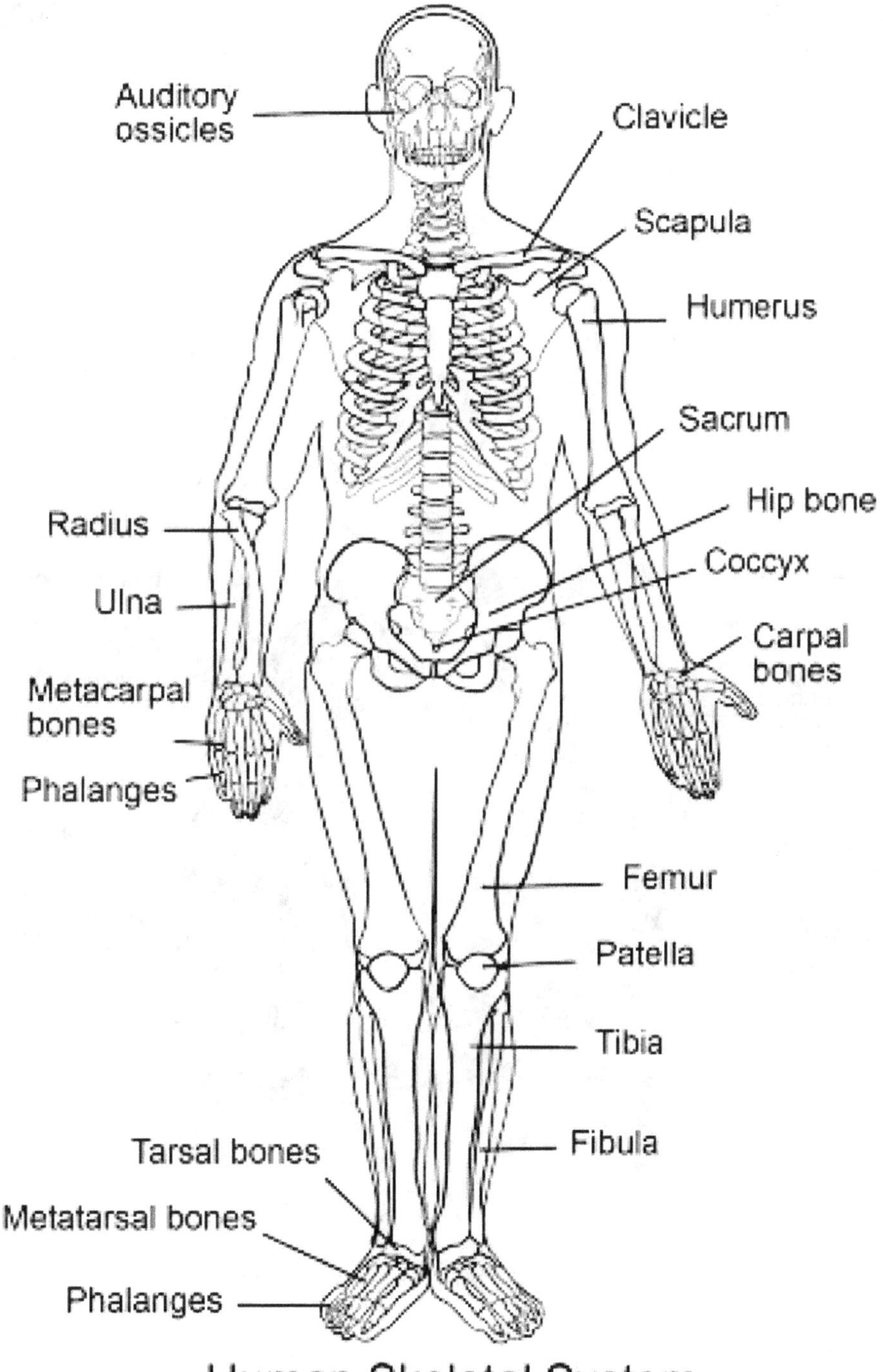

Human Skeletal System

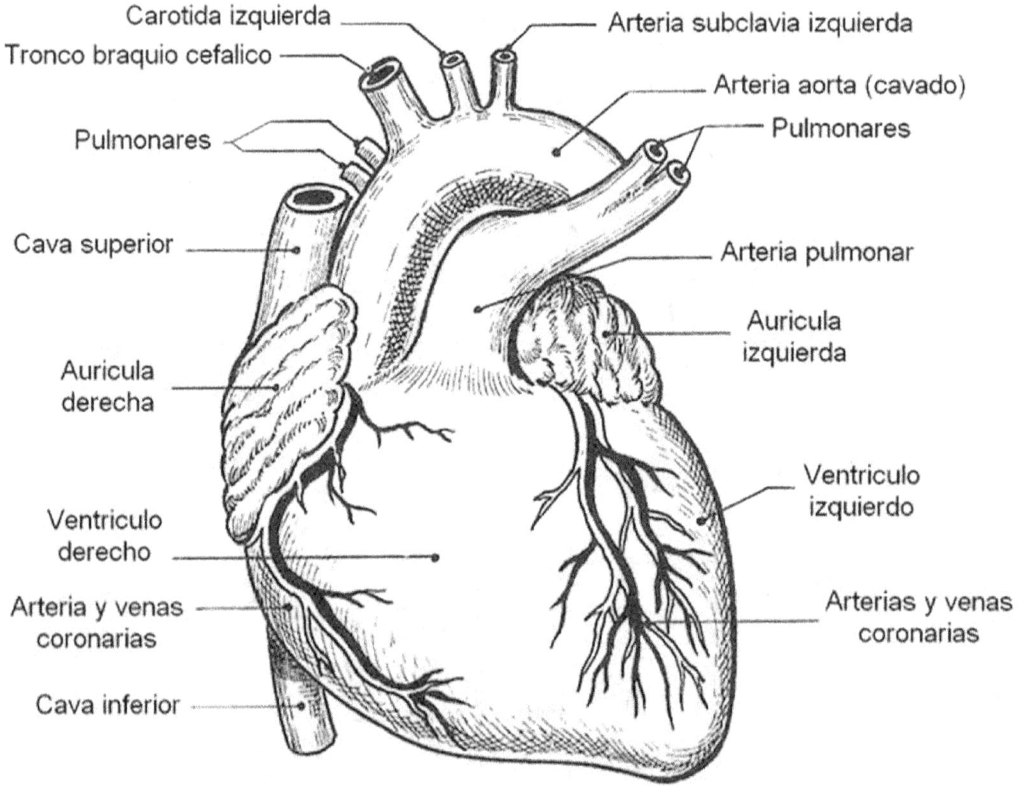

Carotida izquierda
Arteria subclavia izquierda
Tronco braquio cefalico
Arteria aorta (cavado)
Pulmonares
Pulmonares
Cava superior
Arteria pulmonar
Auricula izquierda
Auricula derecha
Ventriculo izquierdo
Ventriculo derecho
Arteria y venas coronarias
Arterias y venas coronarias
Cava inferior

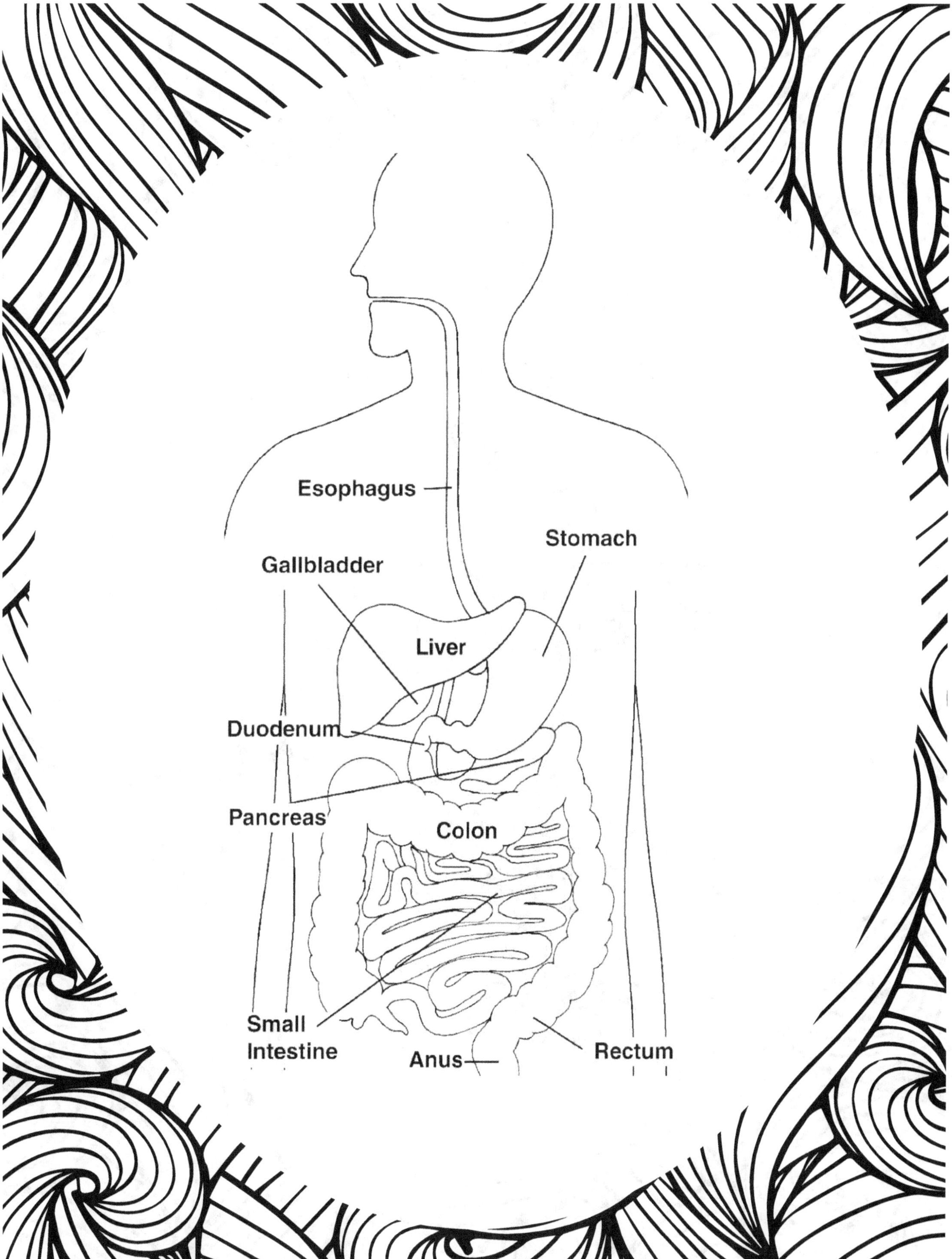
Esophagus
Stomach
Gallbladder
Liver
Duodenum
Pancreas
Colon
Small Intestine
Anus
Rectum

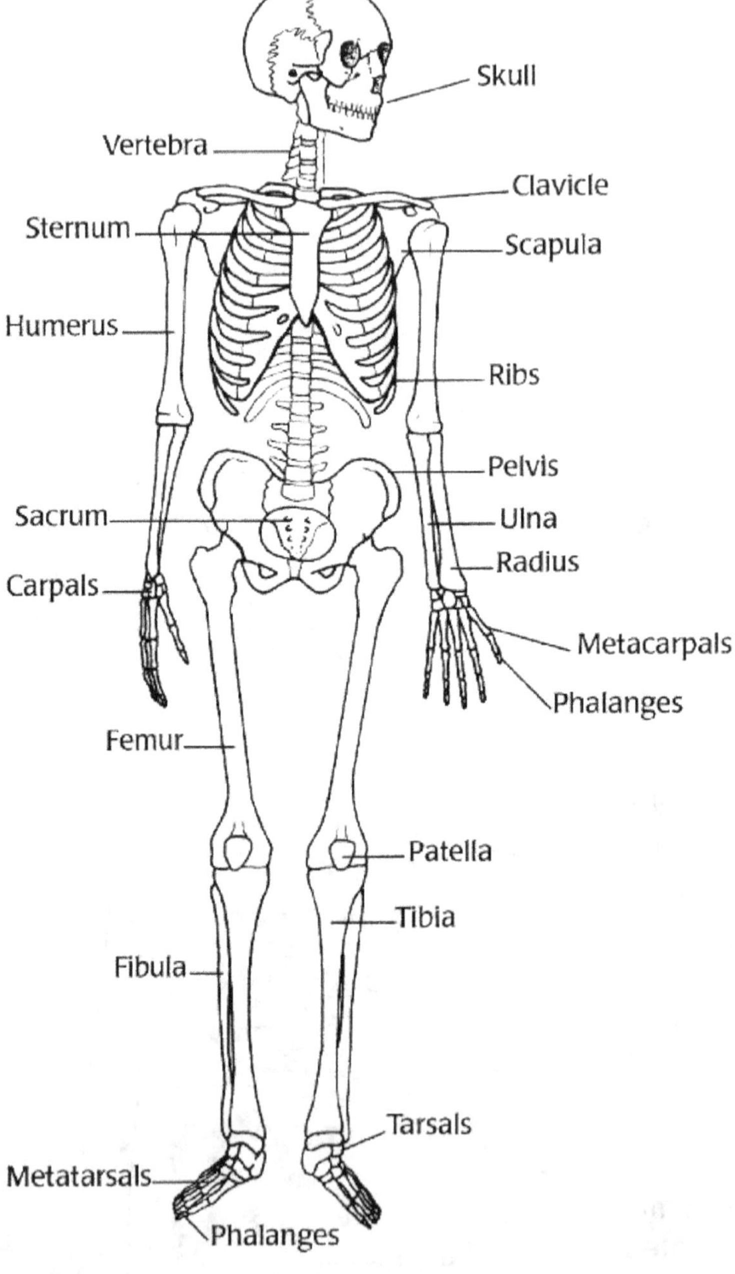
Skull
Vertebra
Clavicle
Sternum
Scapula
Humerus
Ribs
Pelvis
Sacrum
Ulna
Radius
Carpals
Metacarpals
Phalanges
Femur
Patella
Tibia
Fibula
Tarsals
Metatarsals
Phalanges

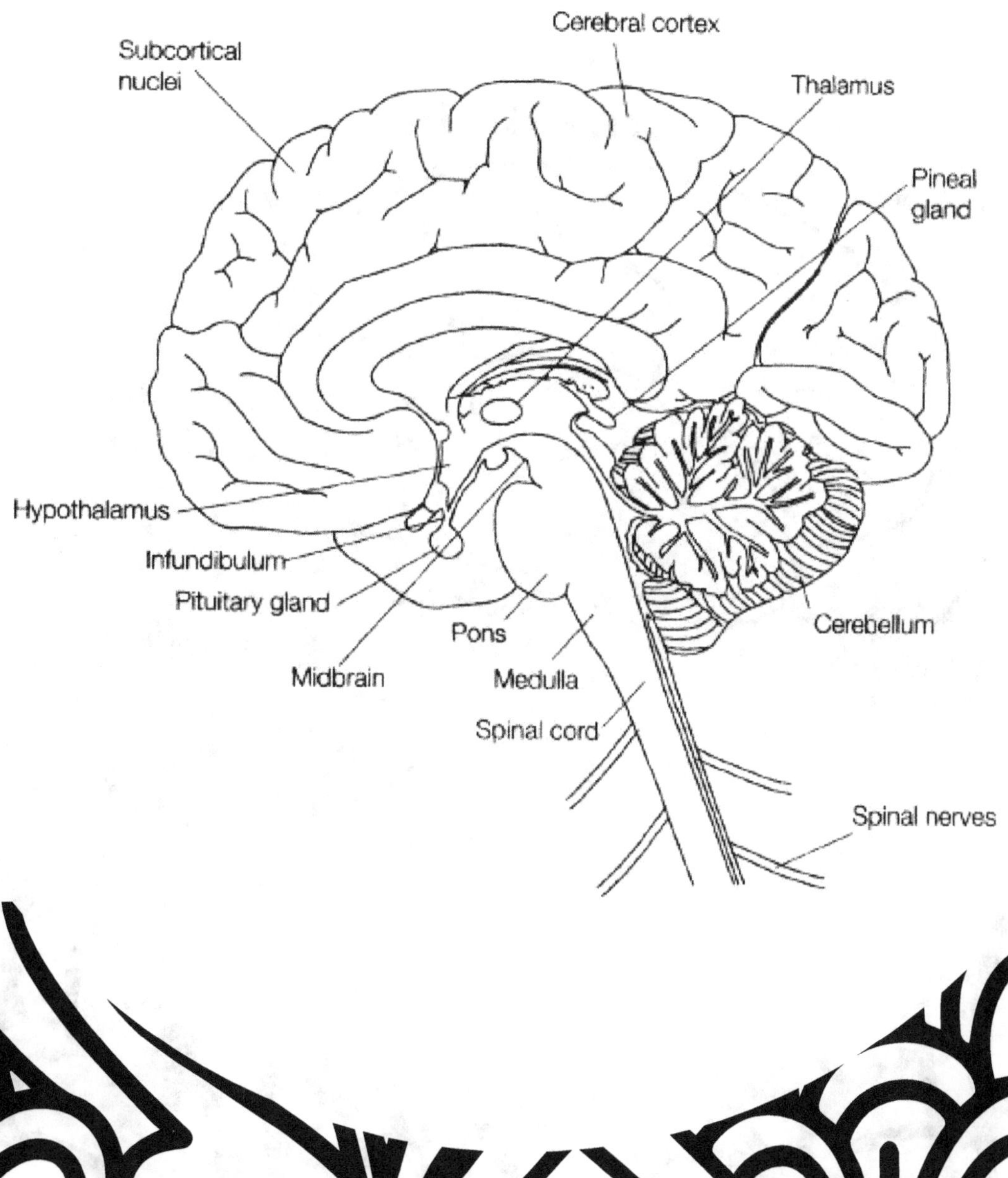

Cerebral cortex
Subcortical nuclei
Thalamus
Pineal gland
Hypothalamus
Infundibulum
Pituitary gland
Pons
Midbrain
Medulla
Cerebellum
Spinal cord
Spinal nerves

The Brain

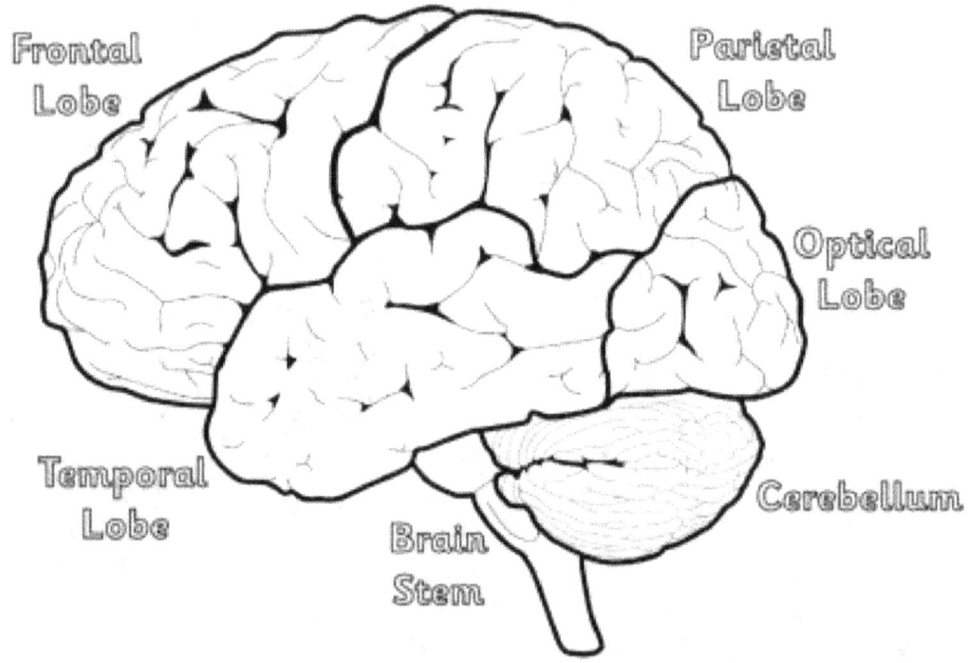
Frontal Lobe
Parietal Lobe
Optical Lobe
Temporal Lobe
Cerebellum
Brain Stem

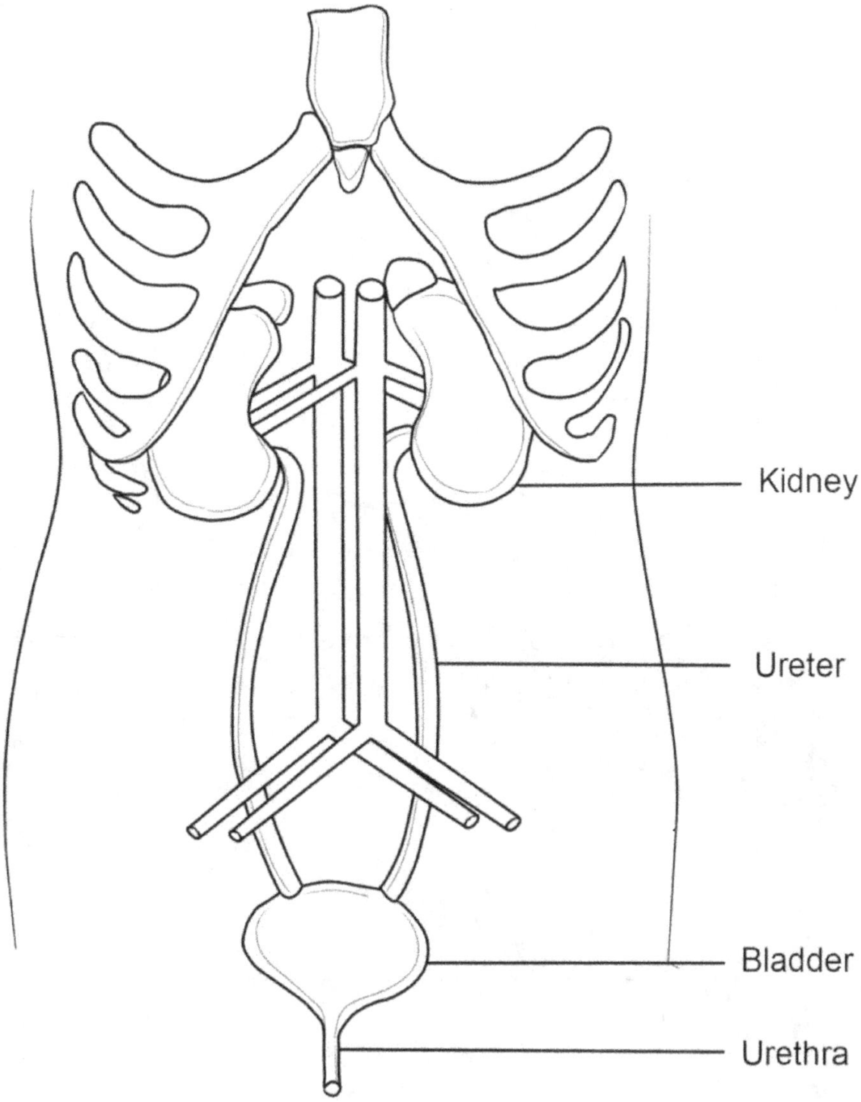

The Urinary System

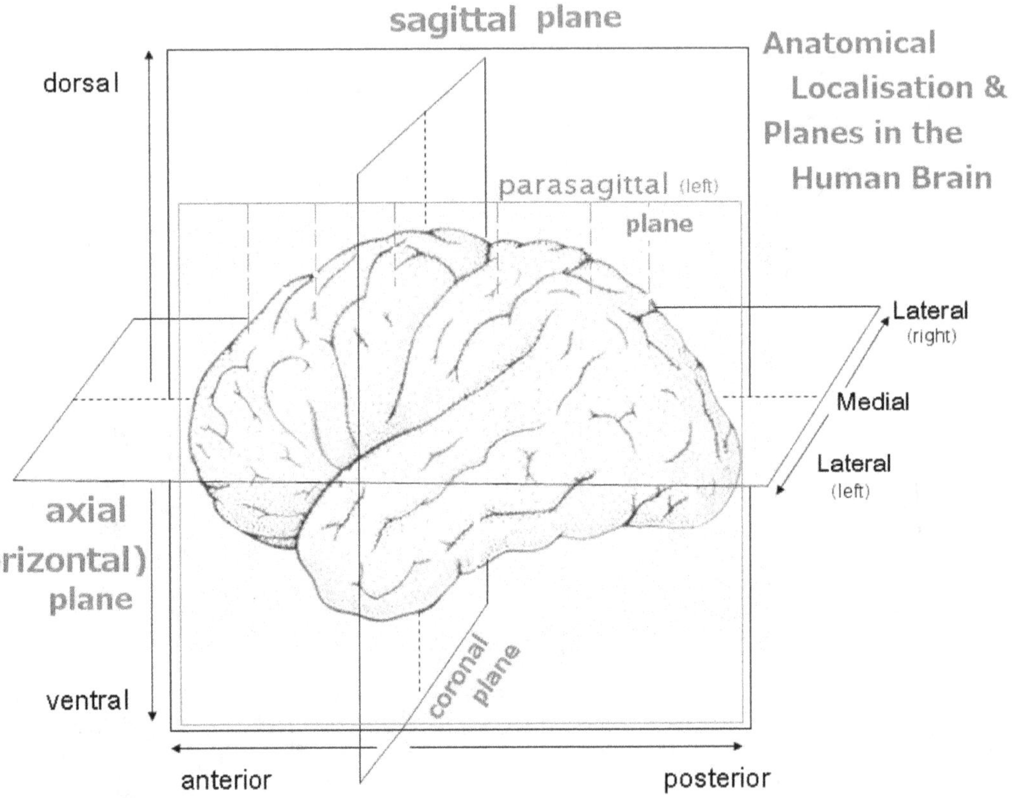

sagittal plane
Anatomical Localisation & Planes in the Human Brain
dorsal
parasagittal (left) plane
Lateral (right)
Medial
Lateral (left)
axial (horizontal) plane
coronal plane
ventral
anterior
posterior

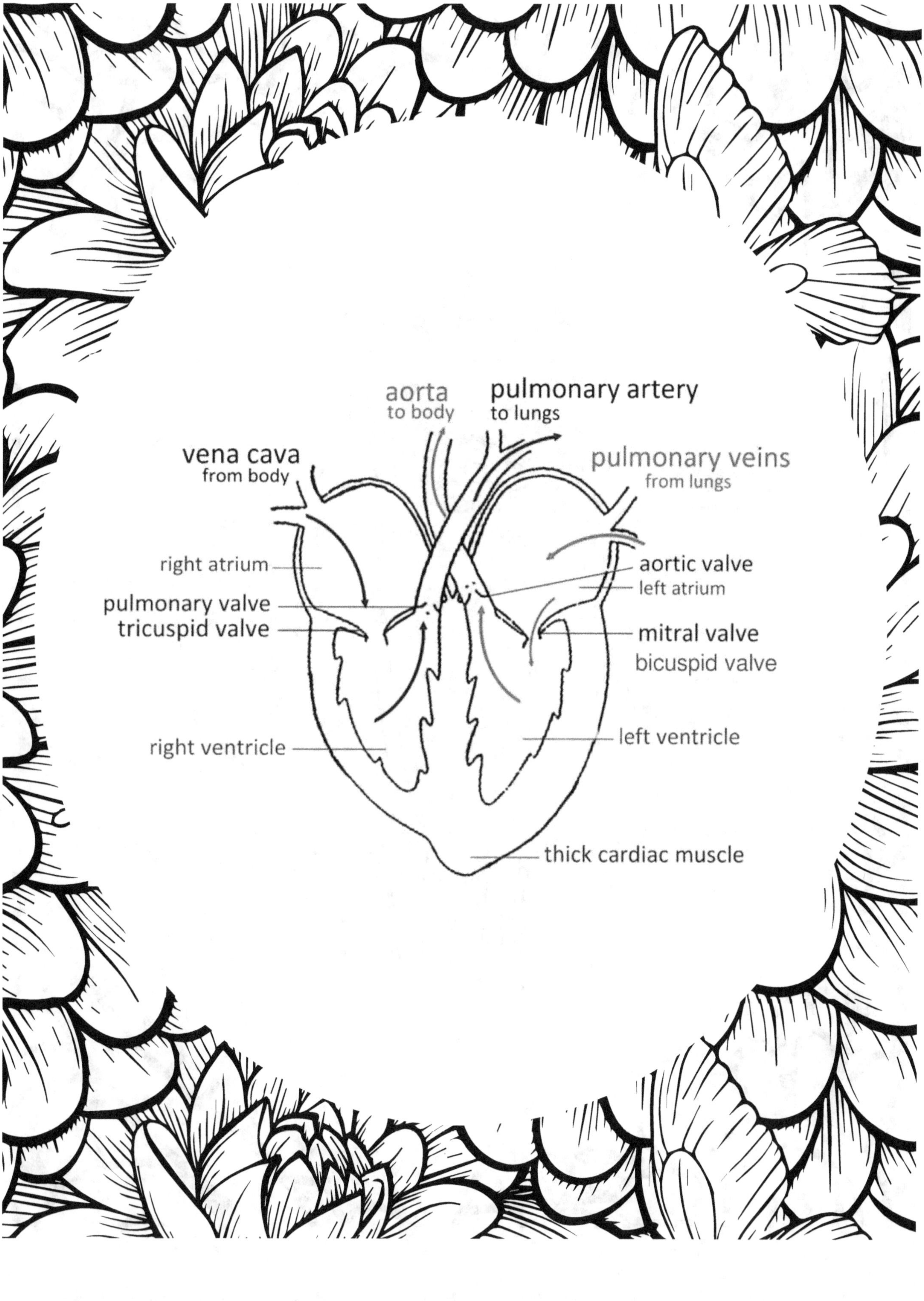
aorta
to body
pulmonary artery
to lungs
vena cava
from body
pulmonary veins
from lungs
right atrium
aortic valve
left atrium
pulmonary valve
tricuspid valve
mitral valve
bicuspid valve
right ventricle
left ventricle
thick cardiac muscle

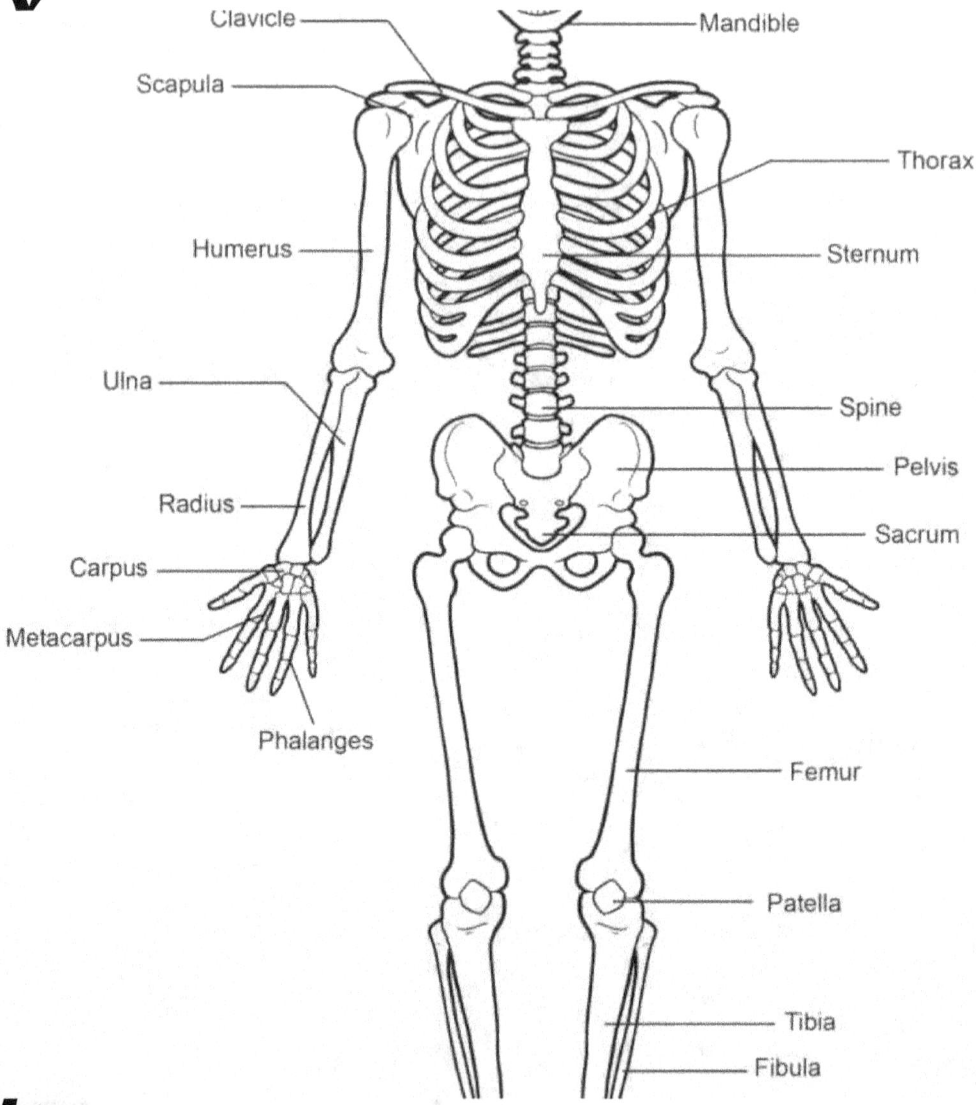
Clavicle
Mandible
Scapula
Thorax
Humerus
Sternum
Ulna
Spine
Pelvis
Radius
Sacrum
Carpus
Metacarpus
Phalanges
Femur
Patella
Tibia
Fibula

www.ingramcontent.com/pod-product-compliance
Lightning Source LLC
Chambersburg PA
CBHW081701220526
45466CB00009B/2840
9798574120606